ECONOMIC ISSUES, PROBLEMS AND PERSPECTIVES

INSURANCE REGULATION

BACKGROUND AND ISSUES

ECONOMIC ISSUES, PROBLEMS AND PERSPECTIVES

Additional books in this series can be found on Nova's website under the Series tab.

Additional E-books in this series can be found on Nova's website under the E-book tab.

ECONOMIC ISSUES, PROBLEMS AND PERSPECTIVES

INSURANCE REGULATION

BACKGROUND AND ISSUES

NELSON R. PHILLIPS
EDITOR

NOVINKA

New York

For permission to use material from this book please contact us:
Telephone 631-231-7269; Fax 631-231-8175
Web Site: http://www.novapublishers.com

Additional color graphics may be available in the e-book version of this book.

Library of Congress Cataloging-in-Publication Data

ISBN: 978-1-62948-141-8

Published by Nova Science Publishers, Inc. † New York

CONTENTS

PREFACE

This book provides an overview of the background and issues relating to insurance regulation, with a focus on insurance agent licensing; federal charter legislation; the Liability Risk Retention Act; the Dodd-Frank Wall Street Reform and Consumer Protection Act; and surplus lines insurance.

Chapter 1 - The individual states have been the primary regulators of insurance since 1868. Following the 1945 McCarran-Ferguson Act, this system has operated with the explicit blessing of Congress, but has also been subject to periodic scrutiny and suggestions that the time may have come for Congress to reclaim the regulatory authority that it granted to the states. In the late 1980s and early 1990s, congressional scrutiny was largely driven by the increasing complexities of the insurance business and concern over whether the states were up to the task of ensuring consumer protections, particularly insurer solvency.

Immediately prior to the recent financial crisis, congressional attention to insurance regulation focused on the inefficiencies in the state regulatory system. A major catalyst was the aftermath of the Gramm-Leach-Bliley Act of 1999 (GLBA), which overhauled the regulatory structure for banks and securities firms, but left the insurance sector largely untouched. Many larger insurers, and their trade associations, had previously defended state regulation but considered themselves at a competitive disadvantage in the post-GLBA regulatory structure. Some advocated for an optional federal charter similar to that available to banks. Various pieces of insurance regulatory reform legislation have been introduced, including bills establishing a broad federal charter for insurance as well as narrower, more targeted bills.

The states, particularly working through the National Association of Insurance Commissioners (NAIC), were not idle following congressional attention.

They reacted quickly to GLBA requirements that related to insurance agent licensing and have since embarked on a wider-ranging project to modernize insurance regulation. This has included both regulatory aspects, such as streamlining the process for rate and form filing, and more basic legal aspects, such as the creation of an interstate compact to provide uniformity across states for some life insurance products. Because enactment by the state legislature is necessary before the legal changes suggested by the NAIC can take effect in that state, the process typically does not move rapidly.

The recent financial crisis refocused the debate surrounding insurance regulatory reform. Unlike in many financial crises in the past, insurers played a large role in this crisis. In particular, the failure of the large insurer American International Group (AIG) spotlighted sources of risk that had gone unrecognized.

The need for a systemic risk regulator for the entire financial system was a common thread in many of the post-crisis financial regulatory reform proposals. The Dodd-Frank Wall Street Reform and Consumer Protection Act (P.L. 111-203), enacted following the crisis, gave enhanced systemic risk regulatory authority to the Federal Reserve and to a new Financial Services Oversight Council (FSOC), including some oversight authority over insurers. The Dodd-Frank Act also included measures affecting the states' oversight of surplus lines insurance and reinsurance and the creation of a new Federal Insurance Office (FIO) within the Treasury Department.

The 113th Congress faces relatively new issues arising from the Dodd-Frank Act, such as the application of federal orderly liquidation authority to insurers (addressed in H.R. 605) and the supervision of some insurers by the Federal Reserve (addressed in H.R. 2140). Congress may also address issues that predate the financial crisis, such as the licensing of insurance agents and brokers (addressed in S. 534 and H.R. 1155/H.R. 1064).

In addition, various international issues may be of concern to Congress, such as the European Union's Solvency II project to overhaul the European insurance regulatory system and general international standards for insurance regulation.

Chapter 2 - The individual states have been the primary regulators of insurance in this country for the past 150 years. Congress specifically authorized the states' role in the 1945 McCarran-Ferguson Act (15 U.S.C. §§1011-1015), and state primacy in insurance regulation has been recognized in more recent laws shaping the financial regulatory system, such as the 1999 Gramm-Leach-Bliley Act (GLBA; P.L. 106-102) and the 2010 Dodd-Frank Wall Street Reform and Consumer Protection Act (P.L. 111-203). The system of multiple state regulators, however, has faced criticism over the years, with frequent focus on the efficiency of the system. One particular aspect of regulation that has been criticized by some as overly burdensome and inefficient is the licensure of insurance agents and brokers, known collectively as insurance "producers." Every state requires specific licenses, sometimes with differing criteria, and insurance producers have identified the need to have multiple licenses as a significant expense for their operations.

Organizations such as the National Association of Insurance Commissioners (NAIC) and the National Conference of Insurance Legislators (NCOIL) create model laws and undertake other steps to harmonize insurance regulation and laws across the country, including the promulgation by the NAIC of models for insurance producer licensing. The individual states, however, are sovereign entities, and any models suggested by the NAIC or NCOIL must first be enacted by state legislatures. The state authorities may amend models or may completely reject suggestions from outside groups. Often this is done with the argument that laws and regulations need to be adapted to particular local circumstances or risks, such as hurricane risks along coastal areas.

Federal proposals addressing multiple state insurance producer licensing requirements through the creation of a National Association of Registered Agents and Brokers (NARAB) appeared as far back as the 102nd Congress, and a version of NARAB was included in the Gramm-LeachBliley Act. These GLBA provisions, known generally as "NARAB I," were conditional, and would not come into effect if a majority of states passed laws providing for uniformity or reciprocity in insurance producer licensing. Although a sufficient number of states met the GLBA requirements and thereby prevented the creation of NARAB, insurance producers continued to identify issues in the state licensing system. As a consequence, "NARAB II" legislation, mandating the creation of a NARAB organization, was introduced in every Congress since the 110th. It was passed by the House in the 110th Congress and the 111th Congress, but was not considered by the Senate.

In the 113th Congress, the National Association of Registered Agents and Brokers Act of 2013 was introduced in both the Senate (S. 534) and the House (H.R. 1155). Under this legislation, membership in the NARAB organization to be created would permit insurance producers to operate in multiple states without obtaining specific licenses from these states. To become a NARAB member, an insurance producer would be required to have a license from at least one state, pass a criminal background check, and meet other requirements to be set by the association. The legislation would require that these additional requirements be not "less protective to the public" than the NAIC model law on insurance producer licensing. The association would be governed by a 13-member board made up of 8 current or former state insurance commissioners and 5 members from the insurance industry. The President would appoint the board, with advice and consent of the Senate, and retain the ability to remove the board and override the NARAB organization's rules or actions. S. 534 was amended and ordered favorably reported by the Senate Committee on Banking, Housing, and Urban Affairs on June 6, 2013.

Chapter 3 - Insurance is one of three primary sectors of the financial services industry. Unlike the other two, banks and securities, insurance is primarily regulated at the state, rather than federal, level. The primacy of state regulation dates back to 1868 when the Supreme Court found in Paul v. Virginia (75 U.S. (8 Wall.) 168 (1868)) that insurance did not constitute interstate commerce, and thus did not fall under the powers granted the federal government in the Constitution. In 1944, however, the Court cast doubt on this finding in United States v. South-Eastern Underwriters Association (322 U.S. 533 (1944)). Preferring to leave the state regulatory system intact in the aftermath of this decision, Congress passed the McCarran-Ferguson Act of 1945 (P.L. 79-15, 59 Stat. 33), which reaffirmed the states as principal regulators of insurance. Over the years since 1945, congressional interest in the possibility of repealing McCarran-Ferguson and reclaiming authority over insurance regulation has waxed and waned.

Particularly since the Gramm-Leach-Bliley Act of 1999 (P.L. 106-102, 113 Stat. 1338), the financial services industry has seen increased competition among U.S. banks, insurers, and securities firms and on a global scale. Some have complained that the state regulatory system puts insurers at a competitive disadvantage. Whereas the insurance industry had previously been united in preferring the state system, it has now splintered, with larger insurers tending to argue for a federal system and smaller insurers tending to favor the state system.

Some members of Congress have responded with different proposals ranging from a complete federalization of the interstate insurance industry, to leaving the state system intact with limited federal standards and preemptions.

A common proposal in the past has been for an Optional Federal Charter (OFC) for the insurance industry. This idea borrows the idea of a dual regulatory system from the banking system. Both the states and the federal government would offer a chartering system for insurers, with the insurers having the choice between the two. OFC legislation was offered in the 107th, 109th, and 110th Congresses.

Proponents of OFC legislation typically have cited the efficiencies that could be gained from a uniform system, along with the ability of a federal regulator to better address the complexities of the current insurance market and ongoing financial crisis as well as the need for a single federal voice for the insurance industry in international negotiations.

Opponents of OFC legislation have been typically concerned with the inability of a federal regulator to take into account local conditions, the lack of consumer service that could result from a nonlocal administrator in Washington, DC, and the overall deregulation contained in some of the OFC proposals.

The recent financial crisis gave greater urgency to calls for federal oversight of insurance and has changed the tenor of the debate. The National Insurance Consumer Protection Act of 2009 (H.R. 1880) was introduced in the 111th Congress by two previous sponsors of OFC legislation. This bill differed significantly from previous OFC bills as it included the creation of a new systemic risk regulator with the power to mandate the adoption of a federal charter by some insurers. The broad Dodd-Frank Act (P.L. 111-203) that was enacted to reform the financial system included some insurance aspects, but did not include a federal charter for insurance. Such legislation has not been introduced in the 112th Congress.

This report offers a brief analysis of the forces prompting federal chartering legislation, followed by a discussion of the arguments for and against a federal charter, and summaries of previous legislation.

Chapter 4 - Risk retention groups (RRGs) and risk purchasing groups (RPGs) are alternative insurance entities authorized by Congress to expand insurance supply through a simplification of insurance regulation. The McCarran-Ferguson Act of 1945 generally leaves the regulation and taxation of the business of insurance to the individual states. In 1981 and 1986, however, Congress crafted a narrow exception to the usual state insurance regulations for these groups, generally exempting them from multiple state oversight. Membership in risk retention and purchasing groups is limited to commercial enterprises and governmental bodies, and the risks insured by these groups are limited to liability risks.

Over the past two decades, interest—both in Congress and in the market—in RRGs and RPGs has varied largely with the vagaries of the regular insurance market. From 2001 to 2004, the insurance market was in one of its periodic "hard" markets, and regular insurance became increasingly expensive and sometimes unavailable. Since 2001, the numbers of risk retention groups rose dramatically and calls have been heard to expand the scope of insurance that they are allowed to offer. At the same time, some problems occurred in individual risk retention groups, and cautionary voices have also been raised. Although the liability insurance market has softened somewhat in the past few years, with policies becoming more available and relatively less expensive, risk retention groups have continued to form in significant numbers.

The fundamental question surrounding expansion of the Liability Risk Retention Act (LRRA) can be posed as an issue of availability vs. reliability. Those who would support expansion often emphasize a failure of the current insurance market and the current regulatory system to make a sufficient supply of insurance available so that consumers who need insurance can find it at a reasonable price. The question they pose is essentially: "What happens to a community when a business, a school, or a doctor can not afford or find liability insurance?" Those who would oppose expansion often emphasize the dangers in allowing insurance to be sold that is not subject to same regulatory standards as "normal" insurance. The question this group poses is essentially: "What happens to a community if the insurer from which this business, school, or doctor purchases insurance ends up insolvent or if the policy does not cover what needs to be covered?" In the 112th Congress, H.R. 2126, the Risk Retention Modernization Act of 2011, would extend the LRRA to commercial property insurance, authorize the Federal Insurance Office to determine the states' compliance with the act and impose corporate governance standards on RRGs and RPGs. Representative John Campbell introduced the bill on June 3, 2011. A similar bill was introduced in the 111th Congress by Representative Dennis Moore, with Representative Campbell as a cosponsor. This report outlines the current regulatory structures affecting risk retention and risk purchasing groups as well as the legislative and market history of these groups. It also discusses the debate regarding possible expansion of these groups into areas beyond commercial liability insurance.

Chapter 5 - In the aftermath of the recent financial crisis, broad financial regulatory reform legislation was advanced by the Obama Administration and by various Members of Congress. Ultimately Congress passed, and the President signed, the Dodd-Frank Wall Street Reform and Consumer Protection Act (P.L. 111-203).

The Dodd-Frank Act largely responded to the financial crisis that peaked in September 2008, but other efforts at revising the state-based system of insurance regulation also pre-date this crisis. Members of Congress previously introduced both broad legislation to federalize insurance regulation along the lines of the regulation of the banking sector, as well as more narrowly tailored bills addressing specific perceived flaws in the state-based system.

The financial crisis, particularly the role of insurance giant American International Group (AIG) and the smaller bond insurers, changed the tenor of the existing debate around insurance regulation, with increased emphasis on the systemic importance of some insurance companies. Although it could be argued that insurer involvement in the financial crisis suggested a need for full-scale federal regulation of insurance, the Dodd-Frank Act did not implement such a federal regulatory system for insurance.

Title V of the Dodd-Frank Act addressed specifically insurance, with a subtitle creating a Federal Insurance Office (similar to language originally contained in H.R. 2609) and a subtitle streamlining the existing state regulation of surplus lines and reinsurance (similar to language originally contained in H.R. 2572/S. 1363). The Federal Insurance Office is to monitor all aspects of the insurance industry and coordinate and develop policy relating to international agreements. It also has limited authority to preempt state laws and regulations when these conflict with international agreements. The act harmonizes, and in some cases reduces, regulation and taxation of surplus lines insurance by vesting the "home state" of the insured with the sole authority to regulate and collect the taxes on a surplus lines transaction. For reinsurance transactions, the act vests the home state of the insurer purchasing the reinsurance with the authority over the transaction while vesting the home state of the reinsurer with the sole authority to regulate the solvency of the reinsurer.

In addition to Title V's specific insurance provisions, various other parts of the act may affect insurers and the insurance industry, including provisions addressing systemic risk, consumer protection, investor protection, and securities regulation.

This report explains how insurance markets were affected by the financial crisis and summarizes the provisions of the Dodd-Frank Act that pertain to insurance.

Chapter 6 - In general, insurance is a highly regulated financial product. Every state requires licenses for insurance companies, and most states closely regulate both company conduct and the details of the particular insurance products sold in the state. This regulation is usually seen as important for consumer protection; however, it also creates barriers to entry in the insurance market and typically reduces to some degree the supply of insurance that is available to consumers. Rather than requiring consumers who may be unable to find insurance from a licensed insurer to simply go without insurance, states have allowed consumers to purchase insurance from non-licensed insurers, commonly called nonadmitted or surplus lines insurers. Although any sort of insurance could be sold by a surplus lines insurer, most such transactions tend to be for rarer and more exceptional property and casualty risks, such as art and antiques, hazardous materials, natural disasters, amusement parks, and environmental or pollution risks.

Although surplus lines insurance is sold by insurers who do not hold a regular state insurance license, it is not unregulated. The sale of this insurance is regulated and taxed by the states largely through requirements placed on the brokers who usually facilitate the insurance transactions. The varying state requirements for surplus lines insurance have led to calls for greater harmonization between the states' laws and for federal intervention to promote uniformity. Such federal intervention is the central focus of the Nonadmitted and Reinsurance Reform Act of 2009 (H.R. 2571/S. 1363), which passed the House by voice vote on September 9, 2009. This act was also added as an amendment to the Wall Street Reform and Consumer Protection Act of 2009 (H.R. 4173) when it was considered on the House floor. H.R. 4173 passed the House on December 11, 2009. The Restoring America's Financial Stability Act of 2010 (S. 3217) included nearly identical language as well. This legislation was reported by the Senate Committee on Banking, Housing, and Urban Affairs on April 15, 2010, and subsequently brought to the Senate floor for consideration. On May 20, 2010, the Senate finished consideration, inserting the amended text of S. 3217 into H.R. 4173 and passing the amended H.R. 4173. The Nonadmitted and Reinsurance Reform Act language was included in the H.R. 4173 conference report, which was agreed to by the House on June 30, 2010, and by the Senate on July 15, 2010. President Obama signed the legislation, now P.L. 111-203, on July 21, 2010.

Provisions aimed at harmonizing state laws regarding surplus lines insurance were also included in the National Insurance Consumer Protection Act (H.R. 1880), whose central focus is the creation of a federal charter for the insurance industry when this bill was introduced on April 2, 2009.

Past Congresses have also taken up legislation on surplus lines insurance. Versions of the Nonadmitted and Reinsurance Reform Act were passed by the House in both the 109th and 110th Congresses, but the Senate did not act on surplus lines legislation in either case. Provisions on surplus lines insurance similar to those in H.R. 1880 were included in the National Insurance Act of 2007, but that bill was not acted on in the 110th Congress.

In: Insurance Regulation: Background and Issues ISBN: 978-1-62948-141-8
Editor: Nelson R. Phillips

Chapter 1

INSURANCE REGULATION: ISSUES, BACKGROUND, AND LEGISLATION IN THE 113TH CONGRESS*

Baird Webel

SUMMARY

The individual states have been the primary regulators of insurance since 1868. Following the 1945 McCarran-Ferguson Act, this system has operated with the explicit blessing of Congress, but has also been subject to periodic scrutiny and suggestions that the time may have come for Congress to reclaim the regulatory authority that it granted to the states. In the late 1980s and early 1990s, congressional scrutiny was largely driven by the increasing complexities of the insurance business and concern over whether the states were up to the task of ensuring consumer protections, particularly insurer solvency.

Immediately prior to the recent financial crisis, congressional attention to insurance regulation focused on the inefficiencies in the state regulatory system. A major catalyst was the aftermath of the Gramm-Leach-Bliley Act of 1999 (GLBA), which overhauled the regulatory structure for banks and securities firms, but left the insurance sector largely untouched. Many larger insurers, and their trade associations, had

* This is an edited, reformatted and augmented version of a Congressional Research Service publication, CRS Report for Congress R43067, from www.crs.gov, prepared for Members and Committees of Congress, dated June 27, 2013.

previously defended state regulation but considered themselves at a competitive disadvantage in the post-GLBA regulatory structure. Some advocated for an optional federal charter similar to that available to banks. Various pieces of insurance regulatory reform legislation have been introduced, including bills establishing a broad federal charter for insurance as well as narrower, more targeted bills.

The states, particularly working through the National Association of Insurance Commissioners (NAIC), were not idle following congressional attention.

They reacted quickly to GLBA requirements that related to insurance agent licensing and have since embarked on a wider-ranging project to modernize insurance regulation. This has included both regulatory aspects, such as streamlining the process for rate and form filing, and more basic legal aspects, such as the creation of an interstate compact to provide uniformity across states for some life insurance products. Because enactment by the state legislature is necessary before the legal changes suggested by the NAIC can take effect in that state, the process typically does not move rapidly.

The recent financial crisis refocused the debate surrounding insurance regulatory reform. Unlike in many financial crises in the past, insurers played a large role in this crisis. In particular, the failure of the large insurer American International Group (AIG) spotlighted sources of risk that had gone unrecognized.

The need for a systemic risk regulator for the entire financial system was a common thread in many of the post-crisis financial regulatory reform proposals. The Dodd-Frank Wall Street Reform and Consumer Protection Act (P.L. 111-203), enacted following the crisis, gave enhanced systemic risk regulatory authority to the Federal Reserve and to a new Financial Services Oversight Council (FSOC), including some oversight authority over insurers. The Dodd-Frank Act also included measures affecting the states' oversight of surplus lines insurance and reinsurance and the creation of a new Federal Insurance Office (FIO) within the Treasury Department.

The 113th Congress faces relatively new issues arising from the Dodd-Frank Act, such as the application of federal orderly liquidation authority to insurers (addressed in H.R. 605) and the supervision of some insurers by the Federal Reserve (addressed in H.R. 2140). Congress may also address issues that predate the financial crisis, such as the licensing of insurance agents and brokers (addressed in S. 534 and H.R. 1155/H.R. 1064).

In addition, various international issues may be of concern to Congress, such as the European Union's Solvency II project to overhaul the European insurance regulatory system and general international standards for insurance regulation.

INTRODUCTION

Insurance companies constitute a major segment of the U.S. financial services industry. The industry is often separated into two parts: *life and health insurance companies*, which also often offer annuity products, and *property and casualty insurance companies*, which include most other lines of insurance, such as homeowners insurance, automobile insurance, and various commercial lines of insurance purchased by businesses. Premiums for life/health companies in 2012 totaled $603.2 billion with assets totaling $5.7 billion. Premiums for property/casualty insurance companies totaled $464.4 billion with assets totaling $1.6 trillion.[1]

Different lines of insurance present very different characteristics and risks. Life insurance typically is a longer-term proposition with contracts stretching into decades and insurance risks that are relatively well defined in actuarial tables. Property/casualty insurance typically is a shorter-term proposition with six-month or one-year contracts and greater exposure to catastrophic risks. Health insurance has evolved in a very different direction, with many insurance companies heavily involved with healthcare delivery, including negotiating contracts with physicians and hospitals, and a regulatory system much more influenced by the federal government through the Medicare, Medicaid, the Employee Retirement Income Security Act of 1974 (ERISA),[2] and the Patient Protection and Affordable Care Act (ACA).[3] This report concentrates primarily on property/casualty and life insurance.[4]

Insurance companies, unlike banks and securities firms, have been chartered and regulated solely by the states for the past 150 years. Legal and legislative landmarks in the state-based insurance regulatory system have included Supreme Court decisions in 1868 (*Paul v. Virginia*)[5] and 1944 (*U.S. v. South-Eastern Underwriters Association*)[6] and federal legislation in 1945 (the McCarranFerguson Act).[7] The McCarran-Ferguson Act specifically preserved the states' authority to regulate and tax insurance and also granted a federal antitrust exemption to the insurance industry for "the business of insurance." (The evolution of insurance regulation is presented in greater detail in *Appendix A*; a legal analysis of the constitutionality of federal regulation of insurance can be found *Appendix B.)*

Since the passage of McCarran-Ferguson, both Congress and the federal courts have taken actions that have somewhat expanded the reach of the federal government into the insurance sphere.[8] The insurance industry has often been divided over the possibility of federal actions affecting insurance. The states typically, though not always, have resisted federal actions, arguing that the states are better positioned to regulate insurance and address consumer complaints and that states have engaged in concerted actions to address concerns raised at the federal level. The two large legislative overhauls of financial regulation in the past two decades, the Gramm-Leach-Bliley Act of 1999 (GLBA)[9] and the Dodd-Frank Wall Street Reform and Consumer Protection Act of 2010 (Dodd-Frank),[10] expanded the federal role in insurance, but the states continued as the primary regulators of insurance following these acts.

GLBA removed legal barriers between securities firms, banks, and insurers, allowing these firms to coexist under a financial holding company structure. Such a holding company was overseen by an umbrella regulator—the Federal Reserve for holding companies that included bank subsidiaries or the Office of Thrift Supervision (OTS) for holding companies with thrift or savings association subsidiaries. Within a holding company, GLBA established a system of functional regulation for the bank, thrift, securities, and insurance subsidiaries. This meant that insurance company subsidiaries within a bank or thrift holding company were functionally regulated by state insurance authorities, with limited oversight by the federal regulator of the holding company. For more information on GLBA, see "The Gramm-Leach-Bliley Act" below.

The Dodd-Frank Act altered the post-GLBA regulatory structure, while leaving the basic functional regulatory paradigm largely the same. The act gave enhanced systemic risk regulatory authority to the Federal Reserve and to a new Financial Services Oversight Council (FSOC), including some oversight authority over insurers. The authority to oversee holding companies, including those with insurance subsidiaries, was consolidated in the Federal Reserve. The Dodd-Frank Act also included measures affecting the states' oversight of surplus lines insurance and reinsurance and the creation of a new Federal Insurance Office (FIO) within the Treasury Department.[11]

Insurance regulatory issues before the 113th Congress include

- overseeing the implementation of, and possible amendments to, the Dodd-Frank Act, including legislation such as H.R. 605, which would remove insurers from the act's orderly liquidation authority, and H.R. 2140, which would address the capital requirements and accounting standards to be used by the Federal Reserve in its oversight of some insurers;

- legislation that would narrowly reform the current regulatory system, such as S. 534 and H.R. 1155/H.R. 1064, which would attempt to harmonize the state regulation of insurance producer licensing; and
- responding to international developments, such as the changes to the European Union's regulatory scheme known as Solvency II and the development of international standards by the International Association of Insurance Supervisors (IAIS).

Recent insurance legislation that has not been introduced in the 113th Congress includes legislation to create a federal charter and regulatory apparatus for insurance (H.R. 1880 in the 111th Congress), remove or limit the McCarran-Ferguson Act's antitrust exclusion for the general business of insurance (H.R. 1583 in the 111th Congress), and expand the Liability Risk Retention Act, or LRRA[12] (H.R. 2126 in the 112th Congress).

LEGISLATION IN THE 113TH CONGRESS

The National Association of Registered Agents and Brokers Reform Act of 2013 (S. 534 and H.R. 1155/H.R. 1064)[13]

The National Association of Registered Agents and Brokers Reform Act of 2013 was introduced in the Senate by Senator Jon Tester along with 13 cosponsors on March 12, 2013. The Senate Committee on Banking, Housing, and Urban Affairs' Subcommittee on Securities, Insurance, and Investment held a hearing on the bill on March 19, 2013.[14] The full committee amended the bill and ordered it reported on June 6, 2013.

Two identical companion bills, H.R. 1064 and H.R. 1155, were introduced in the House by Representative Randy Neugebauer. H.R. 1155 was introduced on March 14, 2013 with 42 cosponsors and additional cosponsors added since introduction, whereas H.R. 1064 has not had additional cosponsors added since its introduction with 41 cosponsors on March 12, 2013. Both bills have been referred to the House Committee on Financial Services.

S. 534 and H.R. 1155/H.R. 1064 as introduced would establish a National Association of Registered Agents and Brokers (NARAB). Apparently because the 1999 Gramm-Leach-Bliley Act[15] included provisions that could have created an identically named association, the current legislation is often referred to as "NARAB II."[16] The NARAB II association would be a private, nonprofit corporation. Its members, required to be licensed as an insurance producer in a single state and meet other requirements, would be able to operate in any other state subject only to payment of the licensing fee in that state, rather than having to obtain a separate license in the additional states, as is often the case now. The association member would still be subject to each state's consumer protection and market conduct regulation, but individual state laws that treated out-of-state insurance producers differently from in-state producers would be preempted. The NARAB II association would be overseen by a board made up of five appointees from the insurance industry and eight from the state insurance commissioners. The appointments would be made by the President, and the President could dissolve the board as a whole or suspend the implementation of any rule or action taken by the association. S. 534 was amended somewhat in committee, but the general structure of the bill remained unchanged.

The Insurance Consumer Protection and Solvency Act of 2013 (H.R. 605)

H.R. 605 was introduced by Representative Bill Posey. It has been referred to the House Committee on Financial Services. Although no hearings directly on the legislation have been held, the bill in a draft form was discussed in a subcommittee hearing in November 2011 and the bill was introduced in the 112th Congress as H.R. 6423.[17] The Insurance Consumer Protection and Solvency Act of 2013 would amend the Dodd-Frank Act so that insurance companies would essentially no longer be subject to the resolution regime created in this law. It would strike the Federal Deposit Insurance Corporation's (FDIC's) backup authority in the case of inaction by state authorities to resolve the insurance subsidiaries of financial holding companies and also exclude insurance companies from the FDIC's assessment authority to cover the cost of FDIC resolution. See "Systemic Risk Provisions" below for more information on this resolution regime.

Insurance Capital and Accounting Standards Act of 2013 (H.R. 2140)

H.R. 2140 was introduced by Representative Gary Miller. It has been referred to the House Committee on Financial Services.

H.R. 2140 would create a presumption that insurance companies subject to Federal Reserve Board supervision[18] are in compliance with the minimum capital standards set by Section 171 of the Dodd-Frank Act[19] if they are in compliance with applicable state capital standards. The bill would permit the Federal Reserve, on a case-by-case basis, to overcome the presumption. To successfully overturn such a presumption, the bill would require the Federal Reserve to have in place and to follow duly promulgated regulations defining the applicable procedures and standards to be followed in determining that an insurance company is not in compliance with state minimum capital standards and to have completed a cost-benefit analysis and a quantitative impact study. The bill also stipulates that governing state law continues to apply and specifies that the Federal Reserve may not require insurance companies that it regulates to comply with any accounting standards differing from those applicable under state law.

IMPLEMENTATION OF THE DODD-FRANK ACT

Federal Insurance Office

Title V, Subtitle A of the Dodd-Frank Act creates a Federal Insurance Office (FIO) headed by a director inside of the Department of the Treasury. FIO is to monitor all aspects of the insurance industry and coordinate and develop policy relating to international agreements. It has the authority to preempt state laws and regulations when these conflict with international agreements. This preemption authority is limited, applying only when the state measure (1) results in less favorable treatment of a non-U.S. insurer compared with a U.S. insurer, and (2) is inconsistent with a written international agreement regarding prudential measures. Such an agreement must achieve a level of consumer protection that is "substantially equivalent"[20] to the level afforded under state law. FIO preemption authority does not extend to state measures governing rates, premiums, underwriting, or sales practices, nor does it apply to state coverage requirements or state antitrust laws. FIO preemption decisions are also subject to *de novo* judicial review under the Administrative Procedure Act.[21] The monitoring function of FIO includes information gathering from both public and private sources. This is backed by subpoena power if the director issues a written finding that the information being sought is necessary and that the office has coordinated with other state or federal regulators that may have the information. In the 112th Congress, H.R. 3559, which would have limited this subpoena power, was marked up by the House Financial Services Committee.

Since the passage of the Dodd-Frank Act, the FIO has hired staff and appointed a director, Michael McRaith, a former Illinois insurance commissioner. The office has been active in international discussions with Director McRaith chosen to head a technical committee of the International Association of Insurance Supervisors (IAIS). The process of starting FIO, however, took longer than some hoped. Mr. McRaith did not take up the position of director until June 2011, nearly a year after the enactment of Dodd-Frank. FIO has released its first annual report,[22] but other reports by FIO to Congress on insurance issues called for in Dodd-Frank have yet to be released.

Systemic Risk Provisions

The Dodd-Frank Act provides for systemic risk provisions that potentially affect the insurance industry through enhanced Federal Reserve oversight and higher prudential standards for all banks with greater than $50 billion in assets, as well as any other firms deemed systemically important financial institutions (SIFIs), and through financial resolution authority to be undertaken by the FDIC. Designation of SIFIs is to be done by the Financial Stability Oversight Council.

FSOC is "charged with identifying risks to the financial stability of the United States; promoting market discipline; and responding to emerging risks to the stability of the United States' financial system."[23] It includes a presidential appointee who is to be familiar with insurance issues, a state insurance commissioner, and the FIO director, with the latter two being non-voting members.[24]

The higher prudential standards may be set by the Federal Reserve based on various risk-related factors. The statutory standards include risk-based capital requirements that account for offbalance-sheet activities, leverage limits, liquidity requirements, risk management requirements, and exposure limits of 25% of a company's capital per counterparty. Other prudential standards may be applied at the Federal Reserve's discretion.

The firms are required to submit resolution plans ("living wills") and credit exposure reports. Regulated subsidiaries continue to be regulated by their primary functional regulator, although the functional regulator may be overridden if the Federal Reserve believes the firm is not adhering to regulatory standards or poses a threat to financial stability. The Federal

Reserve must conduct annual stress tests on systemically significant firms and, in consultation with the FSOC and the FDIC, issue regulations establishing remediation measures to be imposed at an early stage of a firm's "financial decline" in an effort to prevent insolvency and its potential impact on the financial system.[25]

A financial company could be subject to the act's special resolution regime based on a finding that its failure would cause systemic disruption. Any insurance subsidiaries of such a financial company, however, would not be subject to this regime. Instead, the resolution of insurance companies would continue to be conducted in accordance with the applicable state insurance resolution system, although the FDIC would have "backup authority" to resolve insurers if the state system has not acted within 60 days of a finding. With regard to funding for the resolution of systemically important financial firms, there is no pre-funded resolution mechanism under the act. Instead, the FDIC is to impose assessments on financial companies with more than $50 billion in assets, as well as other financial firms that are overseen by the Federal Reserve, to fund the resolution of a systemically important firm in the event the assets of the failed firm are insufficient to do so. The FDIC is to impose such assessments on a risk-adjusted basis. When imposing such assessments on an insurance company, the FDIC is to take into account the insurers' contributions to the state insurance resolution regimes. The FDIC has begun issuing rules regarding the new resolution regime.[26] As detailed above, H.R. 605 would remove insurers from this resolution authority.

FSOC held its first meeting on October 1, 2010, and has begun issuing studies and rules. Of particular significance to insurers was a final rule issued April 3, 2012, detailing the criteria the FSOC would use to judge nonbank financial companies systemically important and require additional oversight by the Federal Reserve.[27]

In general, most insurers have argued that they do not pose a systemic risk due to particular facets of insurance operations, such as the longer-term nature risks faced by insurers, the lower likelihood of runs, and the high capital required by state insurance regulators.[28]

Although FSOC has not publicly stated which companies it is examining for designation as systemically important, two insurers, AIG and Prudential, have indicated that they have received notice of proposed designation as SIFIs by FSOC. These companies retain the possibility of contesting this designation before it is final.[29]

Federal Reserve Holding Company Oversight

The Dodd-Frank Act consolidated oversight of thrift holding companies and bank holding companies under the Federal Reserve. The act also strengthened the capital standards applied to these holding companies, particularly through Section 171, which was originally offered as an amendment by Senator Susan Collins. In tandem with the Dodd-Frank requirements, the Federal Reserve is also implementing higher capital standards for banks as put forth in the Basel III agreement. Although the provisions in Dodd-Frank and Basel III do not affect the business of insurance *per se*, a number of very large insurers, including AIG and State Farm, have depository subsidiaries and now fall under Federal Reserve oversight. In addition to the capital requirements, insurers may also be affected by accounting standards required by the Federal Reserve, which differ from the standards required by state insurance regulators.

The application of Section 619 of Dodd-Frank, commonly known as the "Volcker Rule," could also affect insurers with banking subsidiaries. This section includes restrictions on proprietary trading that potentially could constrain the investment strategies of insurers. The language, however, includes an exemption for trading done "by a regulated insurance company directly engaged in the business of insurance for the general account of the company by any affiliate of such regulated insurance company, provided that such activities by any affiliate are solely for the general account of the regulated insurance company."[30] The transactions must also comply with applicable law, regulation, or guidance. There must be no determination by the regulators that a relevant law, regulation, or guidance is insufficient to protect the safety and soundness of the banking entity or the financial stability of the United States.[31] The FSOC has released a study on the Volcker Rule required by Dodd-Frank, which includes a discussion of the insurance company exemption with a particular recommendation that "the appropriate Agencies should carefully monitor fund flows between banking entities and insurance companies, to guard against 'gaming' the Volcker Rule."[32]

Federal Reserve Chairman Ben Bernanke indicated in July 18, 2012, testimony before the House Financial Services Committee that "we recognize insurance companies have both a different composition of assets and a different set of liabilities, and appropriate regulation needs to take that into account."[33] Insurers, however, have expressed concern that capital rules proposed by the Federal Reserve do not take account of particular characteristics of the industry and describe the rules as "bank-centric."[34]

Several insurers who have operated under bank or thrift holding companies have sought to divest their depository subsidiaries to avoid Federal Reserve oversight and the resulting application of the various rules put forth in Dodd-Frank and Basel III.[35] MetLife is the largest firm to divest its depository subsidiary, although such steps would not prevent the FSOC from designating an insurer as systemically important and thus subject to Federal Reserve oversight from this perspective.

Surplus Lines and Reinsurance

Title V, Subtitle B of the Dodd-Frank Act, entitled the Nonadmitted and Reinsurance Reform Act (NRRA), addresses a relatively narrow set of insurance regulatory issues pre-dating the financial crisis. In the area of nonadmitted (or "surplus lines") insurance, the act harmonizes, and in some cases reduces, regulation and taxation of this insurance by vesting the "home state" of the insured with the sole authority to regulate and to collect the taxes on a surplus lines transaction. The taxes collected may be distributed according to a future interstate compact or agreement, but absent such an agreement their distribution would be within the authority of the home state. It also preempts any state laws on surplus lines eligibility that conflict with the National Association of Insurance Commissioners model law unless the states include alternative uniform requirements as part of an agreement on taxes and implement "streamlined" federal standards allowing a commercial purchaser to access surplus lines insurance. For reinsurance transactions, it vests the home state of the insurer purchasing the reinsurance with the authority over the transaction while vesting the home state of the reinsurer with the sole authority to regulate the solvency of the reinsurer.

NAIC and the National Conference of Insurance Legislators (NCOIL) both developed interstate agreements that would supersede the federal provisions on tax distribution. The two models that were developed, however, differed significantly as to the extent of authority that would be ceded by the states to the new body overseeing the agreement. NCOIL's Surplus Lines Insurance Multistate Compliance Compact (SLIMPACT) is a broader agreement that would address surplus lines regulatory issues and taxes, whereas the NAIC's Nonadmitted Insurance Multi-State Agreement (NIMA) is more narrowly focused on tax allocation. Each approach has been ratified by some states, but most states have ratified neither. This lack of uniformity was addressed in congressional hearings, and representatives of the NAIC and

NCOIL particularly pledged to address the issue, possibly through some sort of blending of the two approaches, before the House Financial Services Committee in 2011.[36] It is unclear, however, how much uniformity has been achieved since this hearing. In the absence of some form of agreement between states, the federal requirement for home state regulation and taxation remains in effect. A 2012 report on U.S. surplus lines insurance by the insurance rating agency A.M. Best concluded that the "overall impression is that NRAA is helping lessen the paperwork load, but intermediaries wish for more consistency between the states."[37]

INTERNATIONAL ISSUES

Although financial services is not an industry that produces a tangible good to be shipped across borders, the trade in such services makes up a large segment of international trade. The United States has generally experienced a surplus in trade in financial services, other than insurance, but in insurance services the United States has consistently run a deficit with the rest of the world.[38] Consolidations in the insurance industry are creating larger international entities with growing market shares, particularly in the reinsurance market. Some have speculated that the growing "internationalization" of the financial services industry means governments may find it difficult to reform their regulation in isolation. The need for a single voice at the federal level to represent U.S. insurance interests on the international stage is a frequently heard argument for increased federal involvement in insurance regulation. The FIO is specifically tasked with developing federal policy in international insurance matters.

International Regulatory Efforts

The International Association of Insurance Supervisors (IAIS) is an international organization made up primarily of insurance regulators from around the world. Its mission is "to promote effective and globally consistent supervision of the insurance industry,"[39] including international standard setting and a variety of guidances and educational efforts. Any standards set by the IAIS would not take full effect until adoption by the sovereign entities with actual authority for regulating insurance. Thus, in some ways, the role of the IAIS could be seen as analogous to that of the NAIC within the United

States. In the aftermath of the financial crisis, the IAIS is coordinating with the Financial Stability Board to identify and suggest policy measures to address global systemically important insurers (G-SIIs). This process is somewhat analogous to the designation of SIFIs by the FSOC within the United States. Both the international standard setting by the IAIS and the G-SII designation process have provoked concern in Congress, particularly the effect these efforts might have on the competitiveness of U.S. insurers and possible weakening of the U.S. regulatory system. The House Financial Services Subcommittee on Housing held a hearing on June 13, 2013, to examine "The Impact of International Regulatory Standards on the Competitiveness of U.S. Insurers."[40]

The European Union and Solvency II

The European Union (EU), the United States' biggest trading partner in insurance services, is implementing a comprehensive program to transform the EU into a single market for financial services. Part of this is an updated solvency regime for insurers—known as Solvency II— attempting to more closely match the capital required by regulators to the risks undertaken by insurers. It is

> an ambitious proposal that will completely overhaul the way we ensure the financial soundness of our insurers. We are setting a world-leading standard that requires insurers to focus on managing all the risks they face and enables them to operate much more efficiently.[41]

The European Parliament first passed Solvency II legislation in 2009. Implementation was originally expected in 2012, with the date then pushed to 2014. Delays in further European Parliament approval have put the 2014 implementation in doubt.

As part of the Solvency II project, the EU created a new European Insurance and Occupational Pensions Authority (EIOPA) with the ability to develop regulations and rules that are binding at a European level, in contrast to the advisory nature of its predecessor. A more efficient regulatory system in the EU could improve the competitive standing of EU insurers compared with U.S. insurers. Concerns have also been expressed that the new EU system might effectively discriminate against U.S. insurers, particularly if state supervision of U.S. insurers is judged insufficiently equivalent to allow the same access to all EU countries that EU insurers will enjoy. EIOPA has published reports on equivalence for Switzerland, Bermuda, and Japan and recommended equivalence for these countries, but has not done so for the United States. There have been suggestions in the past that an EU regulatory change might serve as "a useful tool in international trade negotiations as it could help improve access for European reinsurers to foreign markets," such as the United States.[42] The EU has also cited the overall complexity of the regulatory system in the United States as a barrier to overseas companies operating in the United States.[43]

Reinsurance Collateral

Just as U.S. insurers see access to the EU as a significant issue under Solvency II, access to the U.S. market for insurance is also a significant issue for EU insurers. Of particular concern have been the state regulatory requirements that reinsurance issued by non-U.S. or "alien"[44] reinsurers must be backed by 100% collateral deposited in the United States. Non-U.S. reinsurers have asked state regulators to reduce this requirement to as low as 50% for insurers who meet particular criteria, pointing out, among other arguments, that U.S. reinsurers do not have any collateral requirements in many foreign countries and that the current regulations do not recognize when an alien reinsurer cedes some of the risk back to a U.S. reinsurer. In the past, the NAIC has declined to recommend a collateral reduction, citing fears of unpaid claims from nonU.S. reinsurers and an inability to collect judgments in courts overseas. In 2009, the NAIC put forth draft federal legislation to create a board with the power to enforce national standards for reinsurance collateral, including the reduction of collateral for highly rated reinsurers.[45] In 2010, an NAIC Task Force approved recommendations to reduce required collateral based on the financial strength of the reinsurer involved. This proposal was adopted as a model law and regulation by the NAIC in November 2011. To take effect, however, these changes must be made to state law and regulation by the individual state legislatures and insurance regulators. According to the NAIC, 11 states, collectively representing 40% of the primary insurance premiums in the United States, have adopted revised statutes or regulations with respect to reinsurance collateral reduction.[46] Of the 11 states, however, only Florida and New York have approved any reinsurers for collateral reduction.

STATE REGULATORY MODERNIZATION EFFORTS

Following the passage of GLBA, state insurance regulators working through the NAIC embarked on a regulatory modernization program. These efforts were in response to both the mounting criticisms of state insurance regulation and the recognition of the growing convergence of financial services and financial services products. In early 2000, NAIC members signed a *Statement of Intent: The Future of Insurance Regulation*, in which they pledged "to modernize insurance regulation to meet the realities of the new financial services marketplace." New NAIC working groups were formed addressing issues such as state privacy protections, reciprocity of state producer licensing laws, promotion of "speed to market" of new insurance products, development of state-based uniform standards for policy form filings, and other proposed improvements to state rate and form filing requirements. Highlights of the post-GLBA NAIC efforts include the following:

- Certification of 47 states (as of September 2008) as reciprocal jurisdictions for producer licensing laws,[47] thus exceeding the GLBA requirements to prevent the establishment of NARAB. As discussed above, however, insurance producer groups have continued to raise issues about licensing, and "NARAB II" legislation is being considered by Congress.
- Growth of the System for Electronic Rate and Form Filing (SERFF), intended to be a single, one-stop point of entry for insurers to file changes to rates and forms. More than 544,000 filings were made through the system in 2012, up from about 3,700 in 2001, although the number of filings has fallen since 2010. 49 states participate in the system, which claims an average of a 47-day turnaround for life/health filings and a 28-day turnaround for property/casualty filings over the 12 months preceding April 2013.[48]
- State approvals of the Interstate Insurance Product Regulation Compact. This compact is intended to provide increased regulatory uniformity and a single point of product filing for four insurance lines—life, annuities, disability income, and long-term care. It came into effect in May 2006.[49] Currently, 41 states50 representing approximately two-thirds of the insurance premium volume have joined the compact.

The NAIC maintains that states are better positioned than the federal government to serve the interests of U.S. insurance consumers, emphasizing that state regulators are better suited to ensure that the personal interests of consumers are not lost in the arena of commercial competition. In 2010, according to the NAIC, the total budget for the state insurance departments was nearly $1.3 billion. The states handled more than 304,000 official consumer complaints and 2.1 million consumer inquiries regarding their policies and their treatment by insurance companies and agents. In 2010, the states collectively employed more than 11,600 employees to handle these complaints and perform the other functions of the state insurance departments.

In the aftermath of the financial crisis, the NAIC indicated support for federal efforts to address systemic risk "while preserving State-based insurance regulation,"[51] according to 2009 testimony before the Senate. More recent NAIC testimony before the House detailed several changes in response to the experience in the financial crisis independent of federal efforts. These changes include strengthening the oversight of insurance holding companies through revisions to the NAIC model laws on holding company oversight and increasing oversight on insurers' securities lending, two areas that the experience with AIG during the financial crisis showed to be particularly problematic. The NAIC is also making changes to reduce insurance regulators' reliance on credit rating agencies. In addition, the NAIC launched a "Solvency Modernization Initiative" to examine "international developments regarding insurance supervision, banking supervision, and international accounting standards in order to consider their potential use in U.S. insurance."[52]

APPENDIX A. EVOLUTION OF INSURANCE REGULATION

Insurance companies, unlike banks and securities firms, have been chartered and regulated solely by the states for the past 150 years. One important reason for this is an 1868 U.S. Supreme Court decision.[53] In *Paul v. Virginia*, the Court held that the issuance of an insurance policy was not a transaction occurring in interstate commerce and thus not subject to regulation by the federal government under the Commerce Clause of the U.S. Constitution. Courts followed that precedent for the next 75 years. In a 1944 decision, *U.S. v. South-Eastern Underwriters Association*, the Court found that the federal antitrust laws were applicable to an insurance association's interstate activities in restraint of trade.[54] Although the 1944 Court did not specifically overrule its prior holding in *Paul*, *South-Eastern Underwriters* created significant apprehension about the continued viability of state insurance regulation and taxation of insurance premiums. By 1944, the state insurance regulatory structure was well established, and a joint effort by state regulators and insurance industry leaders to legislatively overturn the *South-Eastern Underwriters* decision led to the passage of the McCarran-Ferguson Act of 1945.[55] The act's primary purpose was to preserve the states' authority to regulate and tax insurance.[56] The act also granted a federal antitrust exemption to the insurance industry for "the business of insurance."[57]

After 1945, the jurisdictional stewardship entrusted to the states under McCarran-Ferguson was reviewed by Congress on various occasions. Some narrow exceptions to the 50-state structure of insurance regulation have been enacted, such as one for some types of liability insurance in the Liability Risk Retention Act created by Congress in 1981 and amended in 1986.[58] In general, however, when proposals were made in the past[59] to transfer insurance regulatory authority to the federal government, they were successfully opposed by the states as well as by a united insurance industry. Such proposals for increased federal involvement usually spurred a series of regulatory reform efforts at the individual state level and by state groups, such as the National Association of Insurance Commissioners and the National Conference of Insurance Legislators. Such efforts were directed at correcting perceived deficiencies in state regulation and forestalling federal involvement. They were generally accompanied by pledges from state regulators to work for more uniformity and efficiency in the state regulatory process.

A major effort to transfer insurance regulatory authority to the federal government began in the mid-1980s and was spurred by the insolvencies of several large insurance companies. Former House Energy and Commerce Committee Chairman John Dingell, whose committee had jurisdiction over insurance at the time, questioned whether state regulation was up to the task of overseeing such a large and diversified industry. He chaired several hearings on the state regulatory structure and also proposed legislation that would have created a federal insurance regulatory agency modeled on the Securities and Exchange Commission (SEC). State insurance regulators and the insurance industry opposed this approach and worked together to implement a series of reforms at the state level and at the NAIC. Among the reforms implemented was a new state accreditation program setting baseline standards for state solvency regulation. Under the accreditation standards, to obtain and retain its accreditation, each state must have adequate statutory and administrative authority to regulate an insurer's corporate and financial affairs and the necessary resources to carry out that authority. In spite of these changes, however, another breach in the state regulatory system occurred in the late 1990s. Martin Frankel, an individual who had previously been barred from securities dealing by the SEC, slipped through the oversight of several states' insurance regulators and diverted more than $200 million in premiums and assets from a number of small life insurance companies into overseas accounts.[60]

Another state reform largely implemented in the late 1980s and early 1990s was the introduction of state insurance guaranty funds.[61] These funds, somewhat analogous in function to the Federal Deposit Insurance Corporation for banks, provide protection for insurance consumers who hold policies from failed insurance companies. If an insurance company is judged by a state insurance regulator to be insolvent and unable to fulfill its commitments, the state steps in to rehabilitate or liquidate the insurer's assets. The guaranty fund then uses the assets to pay the claims on the company, typically up to a limit of $300,000 for property/casualty insurance[62] and $300,000 for life insurance death benefits and $100,000 for life insurance cash value and annuities.[63] In most states, the existing insurers in the state are assessed to make up the difference should the company's assets be unable to fund the guaranty fund payments. This after the fact assessment stands in contrast to the FDIC, which is funded by assessments on banks prior to a bank failure and which holds those assessments in a segregated fund until needed. Insurers who are assessed by guaranty funds generally are permitted to write off the assessments on future state taxes, which indirectly provide state support for the guaranty funds.

The Gramm-Leach-Bliley Act

The 1999 Gramm-Leach-Bliley Act[64] significantly overhauled the general financial regulatory system in the United States. Support for GLBA came largely as a result of market developments frequently referred to as "convergence." Convergence in the financial services context refers to the breakdown of distinctions separating different types of financial products and services, as well as the providers of once separate products. Drivers of such convergence include globalization, new technology, e-commerce, deregulation, market liberalization, increased competition, tighter profit margins, and the growing number of financially sophisticated consumers.

GLBA intended to repeal federal laws that were inconsistent with the way that financial services products were actually being delivered, and it removed many barriers that kept banks or securities firms from competing with, or affiliating with, insurance companies. The result was the creation of a new competitive paradigm in which insurance companies found themselves in direct competition with brokerages, mutual funds, and commercial banks. GLBA did not, however, change the basic regulatory structure for insurance or other financial products. Instead, it reaffirmed the McCarran-Ferguson Act, recognizing state insurance regulators as the "functional" regulators of insurance products and those who sell them.[65]

Some insurance companies believe that in the post-GLBA environment, state regulation places them at a competitive disadvantage in the marketplace. They maintain that their non-insurer competitors in certain lines of products have federally based systems of regulation that are more efficient, while insurers remain subject to perceived inefficiencies of state insurance regulation, such as the regulation of rates and forms as well as other delays in getting their products to market. For example, life insurers with products aimed at retirement and asset accumulation must now compete with similar bank products. Banks can roll out such new products nationwide in a matter of weeks, while some insurers maintain that it can take as long as two years to obtain all of the necessary state approvals for a similar national insurance product launch. In the aftermath of GLBA, the largely united industry resistance to federal intervention in insurance changed. Many industry participants, particularly life insurers, larger property/casualty insurers, and larger insurance brokers, began supporting broad regulatory change for insurance in the form of an optional federal charter for insurance patterned after the dual chartering system for banks.[66]

GLBA also addressed the issue of modernizing state laws dealing with the licensing of insurance agents and brokers and made provision for a federally backed licensing association, the National Association of Registered Agents and Brokers. NARAB would have come into existence three years after the date of GLBA's enactment if a majority of the states failed to enact the necessary legislation for uniformity or reciprocity at the individual state level. The requisite number of states enacted this legislation within the three-year period, and thus the NARAB provisions never came into effect. The issue of insurance producer licensing reciprocity or uniformity continued, as some saw and continue to see problems in the actions taken by the individual states. Not every state has passed legislation implementing reciprocity, and some have argued that it has not always been implemented as smoothly as desired even in those states that did.[67]

Insurance after the Gramm-Leach-Bliley Act

Congress passed the Gramm-Leach-Bliley Act to enhance competition among financial services providers. Though many observers expected banks, securities firms, and insurers to converge as institutions after it passed, this has not occurred as expected. In fact, the major merger between a large bank, Citibank, and a large insurer, Travelers, which partially motivated the passage of GLBA, has effectively been undone. The corporation that resulted from the merger, Citigroup, has divested itself of almost all of its insurance subsidiaries. Although large bank-insurer mergers did not occur as expected, significant convergence continued. Instead of merging across sectoral lines, banks began distributing—but not "manufacturing"—insurance, and insurers began creating products that closely resembled savings or investment vehicles. Consolidation also continued within each sector, as banks merged with banks and insurers with insurers. In addition, although Congress instituted functional regulation in GLBA, regulation since has still tended to track institutional lines.[68]

From the 107th through the 110th Congresses, congressional interest in insurance regulatory issues continued. A number of broad proposals for some form of federal chartering or other federal intervention in insurance regulation were put forward in both houses of Congress and by the Administration, but none were marked up or reported by the various committees of jurisdiction.[69] In the same time frame, a number of narrower bills affecting different facets of insurance regulation and regulatory requirements were also introduced in Congress, including bills addressing surplus lines[70] and reinsurance, insurance producer licensing, and expansion of the Liability Risk Retention Act beyond liability insurance.

Insurance and the Financial Crisis

As the 110th Congress approached its close, the financial crisis that began in 2007 reached panic proportions with the conservatorship of Fannie Mae and Freddie Mac, the failure of Lehman Brothers, and the government rescue of American International Group (AIG) in September 2008. This crisis overlaid a range of new issues and arguments to the previously existing debate on insurance regulatory reforms. The financial crisis grew largely from sectors of the financial industry that had previously been perceived as presenting little systemic risk, including insurers. Some saw the crisis as resulting from failures or holes in the financial regulatory structure, particularly a lack of oversight for the system as a whole and a lack of coordinated oversight for the largest actors in the system. Those holding this perspective increased the urgency in calls for overall regulatory changes, such as the implementation of increased systemic risk regulation and federal oversight of insurance, particularly larger insurance firms. The generally good performance of insurers in the crisis, however, also provided additional affirmation to those seeking to retain the state-based insurance system.

Although insurers in general are considered to have weathered the financial crisis reasonably well, the insurance industry saw two notable failures—one general and one specific. The first failure was spread across the financial guarantee or monoline bond insurers. Before the crisis, there were about a dozen bond insurers in total, with four large companies dominating the business. This type of insurance originated in the 1970s to cover municipal bonds but the insurers expanded their businesses since the 1990s to include significant amounts of mortgage-backed securities. In late 2007 and early 2008, strains began to appear due to this exposure to mortgage-backed securities. Ultimately some bond insurers failed and others saw their previously triple-A ratings cut significantly. These downgrades rippled throughout the municipal bond markets, causing unexpected difficulties for both individual investors and municipalities who might have thought they were relatively insulated from problems stemming from rising mortgage defaults.

The second failure in the insurance industry was that of a specific company, American International Group.[71] AIG had been a global giant of the industry, but it essentially failed in mid-September 2008. To prevent bankruptcy in September and October 2008, AIG sought more than $100 billion in assistance from the Federal Reserve, which received both interest payments and warrants for 79.9% of the equity in the company in return. Multiple restructurings of the assistance followed, including nearly $70 billion through the U.S. Treasury's Troubled Asset Relief Program (TARP). The rescue ultimately resulted in the U.S. government owning 92% of the company. The assistance for AIG has ended with all the Federal Reserve assistance repaid and the sale by the U.S. Treasury of all of its equity stake in the company.

The near collapse of the bond insurers and AIG could be construed as regulatory failures. One of the responsibilities of an insurance regulator is to make sure the insurer remains solvent and is able to pay its claims. Because the states are the primary insurance regulators, some may go further and argue that these cases specifically demonstrate the need for increased federal involvement in insurance. The case of AIG, however, is a complicated one. Although AIG was primarily made up of state-chartered insurance subsidiaries, at the holding company level it was a federally regulated thrift holding company with oversight by the Office of Thrift Supervision. The immediate losses that caused AIG's failure came from both derivatives operations overseen by OTS and from securities lending operations that originated with securities from state-chartered insurance companies.

The 111th Congress responded to the financial crisis with the Dodd-Frank Wall Street Reform and Consumer Protection Act,[72] which enacted broad financial regulatory reform as detailed above. Attention on insurance regulation in the 112th Congress was largely occupied with follow-up to the Dodd-Frank Act. The Dodd-Frank Act left many of the specifics up to regulatory rulemaking, and this rulemaking is still ongoing. Of particular concern was the specific approach that the Federal Reserve may take to bank or thrift holding companies who are primarily involved in insurance and the possibility of FSOC designating some insurers as systemically important and thus subject to additional oversight. Neither issue reached a resolution during the 112th Congress.

APPENDIX B. CONSTITUTIONAL AUTHORITY FOR FEDERAL REGULATION OF THE BUSINESS OF INSURANCE[73]

Pursuant to the Commerce Clause of the United States Constitution,[74] it is generally constitutional for the federal government to regulate the business of insurance because, according to relevant Supreme Court precedent and subsequent decisions explaining the controlling case, the business of insurance is commerce.[75] It therefore may be regulated by the federal government in a manner coextensive with Congress's constitutional authority to regulate any other economic activity with international and interstate aspects.[76]

The authority of the federal government to regulate the business of insurance as interstate commerce was not always clear. The Supreme Court in *Paul v. Virginia* had previously held that "[issuing] a policy of insurance is not a transaction of interstate commerce."[77] The case challenged the constitutionality of a Virginia law that made it more difficult for insurance companies incorporated outside of Virginia to do business within the commonwealth. The insurance industry argued that the statute violated the dormant commerce clause, a legal concept rooted in the Commerce Clause of the Constitution, which prohibits states from discriminating against "foreign" (out-of-state) corporations.[78] The Court found that the Virginia law could not violate the Commerce Clause because insurance was not commerce. In making this determination, the Court appeared to rely on a rather narrow and mechanical definition of commerce.

> These contracts are not articles of commerce in any proper meaning of the word. They are not subjects of trade and barter offered in the market as something having an existence and value independent of the parties to them ... They are not commodities to be shipped or forwarded from one State to another ... They are like other personal contracts between parties which are completed by their signature and transfer of consideration. Such contracts are not inter-state transactions, though the parties may be domiciled in different States.[79]

Subsequent Supreme Court decisions affirmed the holding in *Paul* that the business of insurance was not commerce, and states relied upon this interpretation as they built regulatory systems for the business of insurance.[80]

Seventy-five years after *Paul*, in *United States v. South-Eastern Underwriters Associations*, the Supreme Court ruled differently, holding that the business of insurance is, in fact, commerce and its interstate characteristics may be subject to federal regulation.[81] The case, while not explicitly overruling *Paul v. Virginia*, abrogated the *Paul* decision considerably.[82] *South-Eastern Underwriters* presented the Supreme Court squarely with the question of whether Congress had the power to directly regulate the insurance industry for the first time.[83] In the case, the Department of Justice had brought suit against certain insurance companies for violations of the Sherman Antitrust Act. The insurance companies that were accused of violating the antitrust laws argued that because the business of insurance was not interstate commerce, the Sherman Antitrust Act did not apply to the activities of the companies.

In deciding that the business of insurance is commerce and that it is also *interstate* commerce to which the federal antitrust laws did apply, the majority of the Court took a more practical and less mechanical view of commerce, generally, and the insurance industry, in particular, than the Court in *Paul*. The *South-Eastern Underwriters* Court began by describing the enormity of the insurance business as a portion of the United States economy and noted that many insurance companies operated out of the northeastern region of the country, but did business in multiple states, lending credence to the argument that insurance was, indeed, an interstate commercial enterprise.[84] Furthermore, since the *Paul* decision, other Supreme Court cases had made clear that intangible items, such as contracts not unlike insurance contracts, are items of commerce that can be regulated by Congress.[85] While the Court was willing to concede that "a contract of insurance, considered as a thing apart from negotiation and execution, does not itself constitute *interstate* commerce," the Court found, nonetheless, that "a nationwide business is not deprived of its interstate character merely because it is built upon sales contracts which are local in nature. Were the rule otherwise, few businesses could be said to be engaged in interstate commerce."[86]

The Court concluded its analysis of the Commerce Clause question with a strong endorsement of a broad reading of the powers of Congress to regulate the business of insurance as interstate commerce. "No commercial enterprise of any kind which conducts its activities across state lines has been held to be wholly beyond the regulatory power of Congress under the Commerce Clause. We cannot make an exception of the business of insurance."[87]

Shortly after the decision was issued in *South-Eastern Underwriters*, Congress passed the McCarran Ferguson Act[88] as a direct response to that decision. The first section of the act explicitly declares it to be the policy of the United States "that the continued regulation and taxation by the several States of the business of insurance is in the public interest, and that silence on the part of the Congress shall not be construed to impose any barrier to the regulation or taxation of such business by the several States."[89] The act goes on to ensure state regulatory authority over the business of insurance by preventing federal preemption of state insurance regulations, with some notable exceptions. Specifically, McCarran Ferguson says that "[no] act of Congress shall be construed to invalidate, impair, or supersede any law enacted by any State for the purpose of regulating the business of insurance, or which imposes a fee or tax upon such business, *unless such Act specifically relates to the business of insurance*."[90]

Based upon the emphasized language, it appears that, even within McCarran-Ferguson, Congress has reserved for itself the right to directly regulate the business of insurance when appropriate. And the Supreme Court has upheld Congress's authority to do so. For example, in *Barnett Bank of Marion County v. Nelson*, the Supreme Court held that a federal law granting national banks the ability to sell insurance preempted a Florida statute that forbid banks from selling insurance.[91] The Court reviewed whether McCarran-Ferguson prevented the Florida statute from being superseded by the federal law, and found that because the federal law specifically related to the business of insurance, McCarran-Ferguson's provision preventing state insurance law preemption by federal statute did not apply. In this way, the Supreme Court upheld a federal regulation of the business of insurance, affirming that the business of insurance is commerce under the Constitution, and its interstate aspects may be regulated by Congress.

Congress's authority to regulate the business of insurance under the Commerce Clause extends only so far as Congress's authority to regulate interstate commerce. In the Patient Protection and Affordable Care Act,[92] Congress enacted a requirement for all U.S. citizens to purchase health insurance, commonly known as the "individual mandate."[93] The requirement was challenged by a number of states as an unconstitutional exercise of Congress's powers to regulate interstate commerce. The Supreme Court agreed that the individual mandate was not a valid exercise of Congress's Commerce Clause power in a 2011 decision.[94] In his controlling opinion, Chief Justice Roberts held that while the Commerce Clause granted Congress broad authority to regulate economic activity, it did not grant Congress the power to compel individuals to engage in economic activity.[95] Therefore, though the Chief Justice found that Congress did not have the authority to impose the individual mandate under the Commerce Clause, Chief Justice Roberts ruled in this manner not because Congress does not have the power to regulate the business of insurance, but because the Commerce Clause does not grant Congress the authority to compel individuals to participate in economic activity.[96] While the individual mandate was ruled not to be a valid exercise of Congress's power to regulate interstate commerce, the Chief Justice went on to uphold the individual mandate under Congress's power to levy taxes. [97]

Appendix C. Past Insurance Regulatory Legislation and Proposals

Unenacted Legislation in the 112th Congress

Several pieces of legislation addressing insurance regulation or regulatory requirements were introduced and not enacted in the 112th Congress, including both broad and narrow proposals. This legislation included the following:

The National Association of Registered Agents and Brokers Reform Act of 2011 (H.R. 1112)

H.R. 1112 was introduced by Representative Randy Neugebauer along with 47 cosponsors on March 16, 2011. A similar bill was introduced in the 110th and 111th Congresses and passed the House in each Congress, but was not acted upon by the Senate. H.R. 1112 was referred to the House Committee on Financial Services.

H.R. 1112 would have established a National Association of Registered Agents and Brokers (NARAB). NARAB was to be a private, nonprofit corporation, whose members, required to be licensed as an insurance producer in a single state and meet other standards, would be able to operate in any other state subject only to payment of the licensing fee in that state. The NARAB member would still be subject to each state's consumer protection and market conduct regulation, but individual state laws that treated out-of-state insurance producers differently from in-state producers would be preempted. NARAB would be overseen by a board made up of five appointees from the insurance industry and four from the state insurance commissioners. The appointments would be made by the President, and the President could dissolve the board as a whole or suspend the effectiveness of any action taken by NARAB.

NARAB dates back to the Gramm-Leach-Bliley Act of 1999,[98] and the new legislation is often referred to as "NARAB II." GLBA included the provisional creation of a NARAB to streamline state insurance producer licensing for agents and brokers. The GLBA NARAB provisions, however, were not to go into effect if a majority of the states enacted uniformity in their insurance producer licensing laws and reciprocity for nonresident producer licensing laws. The states met these GLBA requirements. However, some states have not implemented uniformity and reciprocity laws.

The Risk Retention Modernization Act of 2011 (H.R. 2126)

H.R. 2126 was introduced by Representative John Campbell along with Representative Peter Welch on June 3, 2011. It was referred to the House Committee on Financial Services.

This bill would have expanded the Liability Risk Retention Act[99] (LRRA) federal preemption of state insurance laws, allowing risk retention groups (RRGs) to cover commercial property risks and risk purchasing groups (RPGs) to purchase coverage for commercial property risks. The bill would also have changed the enforcement mechanism for federal preemptions in the LRRA and added additional federal corporate governance, disclosure, and fiduciary duty requirements for RRGs under the act.

Under existing law, the federal preemptions in the LRRA are enforced through court action. If a risk retention group believes a state is attempting to regulate in a manner counter to the LRRA, it can bring suit in a federal court. H.R. 2126 would have created a process under which the director of the Federal Insurance Office could issue determinations as to whether a state's regulation of a RRG or RPG is preempted by the act. In addition, the director was to study and issue reports to Congress on the states' regulation of RRGs and RPGs and the compliance with the LRRA.

The corporate governance standards to be issued by the director of the FIO would have included requirements that (1) a majority of directors on an RRG's board be independent, (2) any audit committee be made up of independent directors, written governance standards be in place, and (3) contracts with service providers be limited to less than five years and be approved by the state insurance commissioner. Additional specific amendments to the LRRA would have expanded the consumer disclosure required in the act and imposed a fiduciary duty on the board of directors of a risk retention group.

The Insurance Data Protection Act (H.R. 3559)

H.R. 3559 was introduced by Representative Steve Stivers on December 5, 2011. It was marked up by the Subcommittee on Insurance, Housing and Community Opportunity of the House Committee on Financial Services on December 8, 2011, and approved for consideration by the full committee on a vote of seven to five. The bill was not brought before the full committee prior to close of the 112th Congress. H.R. 3559 was also referred to the House Committee on Agriculture, which did not act on the legislation.

This bill would have removed the Federal Insurance Office's authority to issue subpoenas in its information gathering efforts and exclude insurance companies from the Office of Financial Research's subpoena authority. It also would have extended existing FIO confidentiality requirements that apply to insurance information gathered by FIO to the sharing of such data by FIO or the gathering of such data by federal financial regulators.

The Insurance Consumer Protection and Solvency Act (H.R. 6423)

H.R. 6423 was introduced by Representative Bill Posey along with Representative Judy Biggert on September 14, 2012. It was referred to the House Committee on Financial Services. Although no hearings directly on

H.R. 6423 were held, the bill in draft form was discussed in a subcommittee hearing in November 2011.[100]

H.R. 6423 would have amended Dodd-Frank so that insurance companies would essentially no longer be subject to the resolution regime created in this law. It would have struck the FDIC's backup authority to resolve insurance subsidiaries in the case of inaction by state authorities and excluded insurance companies from the FDIC's assessment authority to cover the cost of FDIC resolution.

Unenacted Legislation in the 111th Congress

Several pieces of legislation addressing insurance regulation or regulatory requirements were introduced and not enacted in the 111th Congress, including both broad and narrow proposals. This legislation included the following:

The Insurance Industry Competition Act of 2009 (H.R. 1583)

Representative Peter DeFazio and five cosponsors introduced H.R. 1583 in the House on March 18, 2009. H.R. 1583 was referred to the House Judiciary Committee, House Financial Services Committee and House Energy and Commerce Committee. No hearings or markups were held on the bill.

H.R. 1583 would have abolished the current exemption from federal antitrust laws for the "business of insurance" that dates to the McCarran-Ferguson Act of 1945 and removed a prohibition on investigations of insurance companies by the Federal Trade Commission. It would not have changed the sections of the McCarran-Ferguson Act that give preeminence to state insurance regulators.

The National Insurance Consumer Protection Act (H.R. 1880)

Representatives Melissa Bean and Edward Royce introduced H.R. 1880 in the House on April 2, 2009. The bill was referred to the House Financial Services Committee, House Judiciary Committee, and House Energy and Commerce Committee. No further action was taken on the bill.

This bill would have created a federal charter for the insurance industry, including insurers, insurance agencies, and independent insurance producers. The federal insurance regulatory apparatus was to be an independent entity under the Department of the Treasury, and the federal law would have preempted most state insurance laws for nationally regulated entities. Thus, nationally licensed insurers, agencies, and producers would have been able to operate in the entire United States without fulfilling the requirements of each of the 50 states' individual insurance laws.

H.R. 1880 also addressed the issue of systemic risk by designating another entity to serve as a systemic risk regulator for insurance. The systemic risk regulator was to have the power to compel systemically significant insurers to be chartered by the federal insurance regulator. Thus, although the bill shared some similarities with past optional federal charter legislation, and would have allowed some insurers to choose whether to obtain a federal charter, it was not purely an optional federal charter bill.

The National Association of Registered Agents and Brokers Reform Act of 2009 (H.R. 2554)

This bill was introduced by Representative David Scott along with 34 cosponsors on May 21, 2009. A similar bill was introduced in the 110th Congress, where it passed the House but was not acted upon by the Senate. H.R. 2554 passed the House on March 3, 2011, and was subsequently referred to the Senate Committee on Banking, Housing, and Urban Affairs, but was not acted upon by the Senate.

H.R. 2554 would have established a National Association of Registered Agents and Brokers (NARAB). NARAB was to be a private, nonprofit corporation, whose members, once licensed as an insurance producer in a single state, would be able to operate in any other state subject only to payment of the licensing fee in that state. The NARAB member was still to be subject to each state's consumer protection and market conduct regulation, but individual state laws that treated out-of-state insurance producers differently than in-state producers would be preempted. NARAB would have been overseen by a board made up of five appointees from the insurance industry and four from the state insurance commissioners. The appointments were to be made by the President, and the President would have had the power to dissolve the board as a whole or suspend the effectiveness of any action taken by NARAB.

The Risk Retention Modernization Act of 2010 (H.R. 4802)

H.R. 4802 was introduced by Representative Dennis Moore (along with Representatives John Campbell and Suzanne Kosmas) on March 10, 2010. It was referred to the House Committee on Financial Services but was not acted upon further.

This bill would have expanded the federal preemption of state insurance laws, allowing risk retention groups to cover commercial property risks and risk purchasing groups to purchase coverage for commercial property risks. The bill would also have changed the enforcement mechanism for federal preemptions in the LRRA, and added additional federal corporate governance, disclosure, and fiduciary duty requirements for risk retention groups under the act.

Under existing law, the federal preemptions in the LRRA are enforced through court action. If a risk retention group believes a state is attempting to regulate in a manner counter to the LRRA, it can bring suit in a federal court. H.R. 4802 would have created a process under which the Secretary of the Treasury could issue determinations as to whether a state's regulation of a RRG or RPG is preempted by the act. In addition, the Secretary of the Treasury and the Comptroller General would have studied and issued reports to Congress on the states' regulation of RRGs and RPGs and the compliance with the LRRA. The corporate governance standards to have been put into place by the bill would have included requirements that a majority of directors on an RRG's board be independent; any audit committee be made up of independent directors; written governance standards be in place; and contracts with service providers be limited to less than five years and be approved by the state insurance commissioner. Specific amendments to the LRRA would have expanded the consumer disclosure required in the act and imposed a specific fiduciary duty on the board of directors of a risk retention group.

The Federal License for Reinsurers Act of 2010 (H.R. 6529)

Representative Dennis Moore introduced H.R. 6529 on December 16, 2010. It was referred to the House Committee on Financial Services but no hearings or markups were held on the bill. H.R. 6529 would have created a federal license for reinsurers. The licensing and regulatory authority would rest with the FIO, which was created under the Dodd-Frank Act, which would have the authority to determine that state laws were inconsistent with federal law and thus preempted.

Administration Proposals

2008 Treasury Blueprint

In March 2008, then-Secretary of the Treasury Henry Paulson released a *Blueprint for a Modernized Financial Regulatory Structure*. Although the financial crisis had begun at that time, the Treasury blueprint was not primarily a response to the crisis, but instead an attempt to create "a more flexible, efficient and effective regulatory framework."[101] A wide-ranging document, the blueprint foresaw a completely revamped regulatory structure for financial services.

The 2008 Treasury model proposed a prudential regulator to oversee the solvency of individual companies, a business conduct regulator to oversee consumer protection, and a market stability regulator to oversee risks to the entire system. As an intermediate step, it made two specific recommendations on insurance regulation. First, it called for the creation of a federal insurance regulator to oversee an optional federal charter for insurers as well as federal licensing for agents and brokers. Second, recognizing that the debate over an optional federal charter was ongoing in Congress, it recommended the creation of an "Office of Insurance Oversight" in the Department of the Treasury as an interim step. This office would be charged with two primary functions: (1) dealing with international regulatory issues, including the power to preempt inconsistent state laws; and (2) collecting information on the insurance industry and advising the Secretary of the Treasury on insurance matters.

President Obama's Financial Regulatory Reform Plan

In June 2009, the Treasury Department under Secretary Timothy Geithner released a whitepaper entitled *Financial Regulatory Reform: A New Foundation*, outlining President Obama's plan to reform financial regulation in the United States.[102] The plan did not foresee as complete an overhaul as did the 2008 blueprint, but it would have substantially changed the financial regulatory system. Specific changes called for included explicitly introducing systemic risk oversight by the Federal Reserve, combining the Office of Comptroller of the Currency and the Office of Thrift Supervision into a single banking regulator, and creating a new Consumer Financial Protection Agency.

Although the June report stated that the Administration was open to additional changes in the insurance regulatory system, the specific regulatory changes called for in the released legislative language were focused on areas other than insurance. Most insurance products, for example, were excluded from the jurisdiction of the new federal consumer protection agency. In general, the states were to continue to have a preeminent role in insurance regulation. Insurance regulation, however, would have been specifically affected through two other aspects of the President's plan: the regulation of large financial companies presenting systemic risk and the creation of a new Office of National Insurance within the Treasury.

Systemic risk regulation as proposed in the legislation would have been the primary responsibility of the Federal Reserve in conjunction with a new

Financial Services Oversight Council made up of the heads of most of the federal financial regulators. The powers to regulate for systemic risk enumerated in the draft legislation extended to all companies in the United States engaged in financial activities. Although the draft legislation did not specifically name insurers as subject to federal systemic risk regulation, it would seem to have included them under federal jurisdiction. Companies judged to be a possible threat to global or U.S. financial stability could be designated Tier 1 Financial Holding Companies and made subject to stringent solvency standards and additional examinations. Such companies would also be subject to enhanced resolution authority rather than standard bankruptcy provisions. Although the draft language did make reference in some places to state functional regulatory agencies, it was left open exactly how the Federal Reserve as regulator of the financial holding company would interact with the state regulators of the individual insurance subsidiaries. Whether federal regulatory deferral to state regulators would have continued under the proposed legislation seemed an unresolved question.

Although systemic risk regulation would likely apply to a relatively small number of insurers, the called-for creation of an Office of National Insurance could have had a broader impact. Unlike the similarly named office in other legislation, such as H.R. 1880 in the 111th Congress, President Obama's Office of National Insurance would not have overseen a federal insurance charter or have had direct regulatory power over insurers. Rather, this office was to operate as a broad overseer and voice for insurance at the federal level, including collecting information on insurance issues, setting federal policy on insurance, representing the United States in international insurance matters, and preempting some state laws where these laws are inconsistent with international agreements.

End Notes

[1] Premium amounts used are net premiums written and asset amounts are admitted assets from AM Best, Statistical Study: U.S. Property/Casualty - 2012 Financial Results, March 25, 2013, and AM Best, Statistical Study: U.S. Life/Health - 2012 Financial Results, March 25, 2013.

[2] P.L. 93-406, 88 Stat. 829.

[3] P.L. 111-148, 124 Stat. 119.

[4] For more information on health insurance, see CRS Report RL32237, Health Insurance: A Primer, by Bernadette Fernandez.

[5] Paul v. Virginia, 75 U.S. (8 Wall.) 168 (1868).

[6] U.S. v. South-Eastern Underwriters Association, 322 U.S. 533 (1944).

[7] Codified at 15 U.S.C. § 1011 et seq.

[8] For more information on court decisions, see CRS Report RL33683, Courts Narrow McCarran-Ferguson Antitrust Exemption for "Business of Insurance": Viability of "State Action" Doctrine as an Alternative, by Janice E. Rubin.

[9] P.L. 106-102, 113 Stat. 1338.

[10] P.L. 111-203, 124 Stat. 1376.

[11] For more information on the specific insurance provisions in the Dodd-Frank Act, see CRS Report R41372, The Dodd-Frank Wall Street Reform and Consumer Protection Act: Insurance Provisions, by Baird Webel.

[12] 15 U.S.C. § 3901 et seq. See CRS Report RL32176, The Liability Risk Retention Act: Background, Issues, and Current Legislation, by Baird Webel.

[13] For more information, please see CRS Report R43095, Insurance Agent Licensing: Overview and Background on Federal "NARAB" Legislation, by Baird Webel.

[14] Hearing webcast and statements can be found at http://www.banking.senate.gov /public/ index.cfm?FuseAction=Hearings.Hearing&Hearing_ID=72d49be4-ff44-4d01-862a-4654e 13b2589.

[15] Specifically, P.L. 106-102, Title III, Subtitle C. See the discussion below under "The Gramm-Leach-Bliley Act."

[16] GLBA included the provisional creation of a NARAB to streamline state insurance producer licensing for agents and brokers. The GLBA NARAB provisions, however, were not to go into effect if a majority of the states enacted uniformity in their insurance producer licensing laws and reciprocity for nonresident producer licensing laws. The states as a whole met these GLBA requirements, but some individual states never adopted reciprocity legislation.

[17] See U.S. Congress, House Committee on Financial Services, Subcommittee on Insurance, Housing and Community Opportunity, Insurance Oversight and Legislative Proposals, 112th Cong., 1st sess., November 16, 2011, http://financialservices.house.gov/calendar/ eventsingle.aspx?EventID=268154.

[18] This would include insurers who are part of bank holding companies or savings and loan holding companies and insurers designated as systemically significant financial institutions by FSOC.

[19] Codified at 12 U.S.C. § 5371.

[20] 31 U.S.C. § 313(r)(2) as added by P.L. 111-203 § 502; the law renumbers the current 31 U.S.C. § 313 as 31 U.S.C. § 312.

[21] 5 U.S.C. § 551 et seq.

[22] This report can be found at http://www.treasury.gov/initiatives/fio/reports-and-notices/ Documents/ FIO%20Annual%20Report%202013.pdf.

[23] See the FSOC website at http://www.treasury.gov/initiatives/fsoc/Pages/home.aspx.

[24] For more information on the FSOC, see CRS Report R42083, Financial Stability Oversight Council: A Framework to Mitigate Systemic Risk, by Edward V. Murphy.

[25] This information adapted from CRS Report R41384, The Dodd-Frank Wall Street Reform and Consumer Protection Act: Systemic Risk and the Federal Reserve, by Marc Labonte.

[26] Information on the FDIC's role in implementing Dodd-Frank can be found at http://www. fdic.gov/regulations/ reform/.

[27] Text of the final rule can be found on the FSOC website at http://www.treasury.gov/ initiatives/ fsoc/Documents/Nonbank%20Designations%20-%20Final%20Rule% 20and%20Guidance. pdf.

[28] See, for example, comments submitted on the FSOC rule by the American Council of Life Insurers and the Property and Casualty Insurers Coalition, available at http://www. regu

lations.gov/#!documentDetail;D=FSOC-2011-0001-0024 and http://www.regulations.gov/#!documentDetail; D=FSOC-2011-0001-0023.

[29] See, for example, Prudential Financial, Inc. "Form 8-K," filed with the Securities and Exchange Commission on June 3, 2013.

[30] P.L. 111-203 § 619(d)(1)(F).

[31] This description is from CRS Report R41298, The "Volcker Rule": Proposals to Limit "Speculative" Proprietary Trading by Banks, by David H. Carpenter and M. Maureen Murphy; please see this report for additional information on the proposal.

[32] Financial Stability Oversight Council, Study & Recommendations On Prohibitions On Proprietary Trading & Certain Relationships With Hedge Funds & Private Equity Funds, January 2011, pp. 71-75.

[33] See Chairman Bernanke's response to questioning from Rep. Judy Biggert in the archived hearing webcast at http://financialservices.house.gov/calendar/ eventsingle.aspx?EventID =302778, beginning at approximately 1:54.

[34] Comments can be found at http://www.federalreserve.gov/apps/foia/ViewComments.aspx?doc_id=R-1442& doc_ver=1, see, for example, page 25 of the State Farm comment letter at http://www.federalreserve.gov/SECRS/2012/ October/20121025/R-1442/R-1442_101912_109851_308150202515_1.pdf.

[35] See, for example, SNL Financial, "Another insurer-owned bank seeks Shelter from oncoming regulatory storm," November 6, 2012, available at http://www.snl.com/InteractiveX /article.aspx?CDID=A-16216891-11568&KPLT=2.

[36] See U.S. Congress, House Committee on Financial Services, Subcommittee on Insurance, Housing and Community Opportunity, Insurance Oversight: Policy Implications for U.S. Consumers, Businesses and Jobs, 112th Cong., 1st sess., July 28, 2011, particularly the statements by Mr. Clay Jackson and Ms. Letha E. Heaton, available at http://financia lservices.house.gov/Calendar/EventSingle.aspx?EventID=252895.

[37] A.M. Best, "2012 Special Report: U.S. Surplus Lines – Market Review. Domestic Surplus Lines Insurers Reverse Downward Trend," October 1, 2012, p. 32.

[38] In 2011, U.S. exports of non-insurance financial services were $74.1 billion in 2011 versus imports of $16.2 billion compared with insurance exports that totaled $15.5 billion versus imports of $56.6 billion. See the Bureau of Economic Analysis website at http://www.bea.gov/iTable/iTable.cfm?ReqID=6&step=1, Table 3a.

[39] From the IAIS website at http://www.iaisweb.org/About-the-IAIS-28.

[40] For hearing webcast and transcripts, see http://financialservices.house.gov/calendar/ eventsingle.aspx?EventID= 337125.

[41] Charlie McCreevy, European Union Internal Market and Services Commissioner, quoted in "'Solvency II': EU to take global lead in insurance regulation" available at http://europa.eu/rapid/pressReleasesAction.do?reference=IP/07/ 1060&format=HTML&aged=0&language=EN&guiLanguage=en. The general EU website on Solvency 2 is http://ec.europa.eu/internal_market/insurance/solvency/index_en.htm.

[42] European Commission, "Commission Proposes a Directive to Create a Real EU-Wide Market for Reinsurance," Internal Market: Financial Services: Insurance: Press Release, April 21, 2004, at http://europa.eu/rapid/ pressReleasesAction.do?reference=IP/04/ 513&format=PDF&aged=1&language=EN&guiLanguage=en.

[43] See, for example, p. 54 of the European Commission's US Barriers to Trade and Investment Report for 2007, at http://trade.ec.europa.eu/doclib/docs/2008/april/tradoc_138559.pdf.pdf.

[44] In the United States, the term "foreign" insurer generally denotes an insurer that is chartered in a different state; those insurers from a different country have been called "alien" insurers.

[45] The NAIC proposal can be found on their website at http://www.naic.org/committees _e_reinsurance.htm.

[46] These states include California, Connecticut, Delaware, Florida, Georgia, Indiana, Louisiana, New Jersey, New York, Pennsylvania, and Virginia.

[47] See http://www.naic.org/urtt_utlr.htm.

[48] See http://www.serff.org/about.htm.

[49] See http://www.insurancecompact.org.

[50] AK, AL, CO, GA, HI, IA, ID, IL, IN, KS, KY, LA, MA, MD, ME, MI, MN, MO, MS, NC, NE, NH, NJ, NM, NV, OH, OK, OR, PA, RI, SC, TN, TX, UT, VA, VT, WA, WI, WV, and WY. Puerto Rico is also a member.

[51] Prepared Testimony of The Honorable Michael T. McRaith in U.S. Congress, Senate Committee on Banking, Housing, and Urban Affairs, Perspectives on Modernizing Insurance Regulation, 111th Cong., 1st sess., March 17, 2009, available at http://banking.senate.gov/public/index.cfm?FuseAction=Files.View&FileStore_id=9d32d178-0b51- 415d-989d-8bd87d6477e0.

[52] Prepared Testimony of Iowa Insurance Commissioner Susan E. Voss in U.S. Congress, House Committee on Financial Services, Subcommittee on Insurance, Housing and Community Opportunity, Insurance Oversight: Policy Implications for U.S. Consumers, Businesses and Jobs, 112th Cong., 1st sess., July 28, 2011, available at http://financialservices.house.gov/UploadedFiles/072811voss.pdf. See also http://naic.org/index_smi.htm.

[53] Paul v. Virginia, 75 U.S. (8 Wall.) 168 (1868).

[54] U.S. v. South-Eastern Underwriters Association, 322 U.S. 533 (1944).

[55] 15 U.S.C. § 1011 et seq.

[56] Richard Cordero, Exemption or Immunity from Federal Antitrust Liability Under McCarran-Ferguson (15 U.S.C. 1011-1013) and State Action and Noer-Pennington Doctrines for Business of Insurance and Persons Engaged in It, 116 ALR Fed 163, 194 (1993).

[57] 15 U.S.C. § 1012(b). The Supreme Court has made clear that the business of insurance does not include all business of insurers in Group Health and Life Insurance, Co. v. Royal Drug, Co., 440 U.S. 205, 279 (1979). For further explanation of this distinction, see the CRS Report RL33683, Courts Narrow McCarran-Ferguson Antitrust Exemption for "Business of Insurance": Viability of "State Action" Doctrine as an Alternative, by Janice E. Rubin.

[58] 15 U.S.C. § 3901 et seq. See CRS Report RL32176, The Liability Risk Retention Act: Background, Issues, and Current Legislation, by Baird Webel.

[59] Most such proposals prior to the 1990s focused on relatively narrow amendments to McCarran-Ferguson rather than large-scale replacement of the state regulatory system.

[60] See, for example, "17-Year Sentence Affirmed for Investor Who Looted Insurers," New York Times, March 24, 2006, available at http://www.nytimes.com/2006/03/24frankel. .html?ref=martinfrankel.

[61] For more information, see CRS Report RL32175, Insurance Guaranty Funds, by Baird Webel.

[62] National Conference of Insurance Guaranty Funds, "Facts and Statistics," available at http://www.ncigf.org/mediafacts.

[63] National Organization of Life & Health Insurance Guaranty Associations, "Frequently Asked Questions," available at http://www.nolhga.com/policyholderinfo/main. cfm/location/questions.

[64] P.L. 106-102, 113 Stat. 1338.

[65] Functional regulation would entail, for example, insurance regulators overseeing insurance products being offered by banks, while banking regulators would oversee banking products offered by insurers. Institutional regulation tends to focus on the charter of the institution;

for example, banking regulators oversee all the activities of a bank even if the bank is offering insurance products.

[66] Banking charters are available from both the individual states and the federal government. For more information on optional federal charter legislation, see CRS Report RL34286, Insurance Regulation: Federal Charter Legislation, by Baird Webel.

[67] See, for example, the April 16, 2008, testimony by Tom Minkler on behalf of the Independent Insurance Agents and Brokers made before the House Financial Services Subcommittee on Capital Markets, Insurance, and Government Sponsored Enterprises at http://www.house.gov/apps/list/hearing/financialsvcs_dem/minkler041608.pdf.

[68] See CRS Report RS21827, Insurance Regulation After the Gramm-Leach-Bliley Act, by Carolyn Cobb.

[69] Broad proposals from the 107th to 110th Congresses included the National Insurance Act of 2007 (S. 40 and H.R. 3200, 110th Congress); the National Insurance Act of 2006 (S. 2509 and H.R. 6225, 109th Congress); the Insurance Consumer Protection Act of 2003 (S. 1373, 108th Congress); and the Insurance Industry Modernization and Consumer Protection Act (H.R. 3766, 107th Congress), and the 2008 Blueprint for a Modernized Financial Regulatory Structure released by the U.S. Treasury and available at http://www.treasury.gov/press-center/press-releases/Documents/ Blueprint.pdf.

[70] Surplus lines insurance is insurance sold by insurance companies not licensed in the particular state where it is sold. For background on this insurance, see CRS Report RS22506, Surplus Lines Insurance: Background and Current Legislation, by Baird Webel.

[71] See CRS Report R42953, Government Assistance for AIG: Summary and Cost, by Baird Webel and CRS Report R40438, Federal Government Assistance for American International Group (AIG), by Baird Webel.

[72] P.L. 111-203, 124 Stat. 1376. See CRS Report R41350, The Dodd-Frank Wall Street Reform and Consumer Protection Act: Issues and Summary, coordinated by Baird Webel.

[73] This appendix authored by CRS Legislative Attorney Kathleen Ruane.

[74] U.S. Const., Art. I, § 8, cl. 3. ("The Congress shall have Power ... To regulate Commerce with foreign Nations, and among the several States, and with the Indian Tribes."). For a general discussion of Congress's Commerce Clause Powers, see CRS Report RL32844, The Power to Regulate Commerce: Limits on Congressional Power, by Kenneth R. Thomas.

[75] United States v. South-Eastern Underwriters Assoc., 322 U.S. 533 (1944).

[76] Id.

[77] 75 U.S. 168, 183 (1869).

[78] Okla. Tax Comm'n v. Jefferson Lines, 514 U.S. 175, 180 (1995) (The dormant commerce clause "prevent[s] a State from retreating into economic isolation or jeopardizing the welfare of the Nation as a whole, as it would do if it were free to place burdens on the flow of commerce across its borders that commerce wholly within those borders would not bear.").

[79] Paul v. Virginia, 75 U.S. at 183.

[80] See, e.g., Hooper v. California, 155 U.S. 648 (1895) ("The business of insurance is not commerce."); New York Life Ins. Co. v. Deer Lodge County, 231 U.S. 495 (1913) ("Contracts of insurance are not commerce.").

[81] 322 U.S. 533 (1944).

[82] It appears that South-Eastern Underwriters did not explicitly overrule Paul v. Virginia because Paul v. Virginia presented a question regarding the limits of state authority under the commerce clause; whereas South-Eastern Underwriters presented a question regarding the

authority of Congress to regulate the business of insurance as interstate commerce. 322 U.S. at 544.

[83] Id.

[84] Id. at 539-543.

[85] Id. at 546.

[86] Id. at 547.

[87] Id. at 553. It is worth noting that the decision in South-Eastern Underwriters was not a unanimous one. The case was decided 4-3. However, two of the dissenting Justices in the case explicitly agreed with the majority that Congress could regulate the insurance industry to the same extent that it could regulate other industries in interstate commerce. Id. at 562-63 (J.Stone, dissenting); Id. at 583 (J. Frankfurter, dissenting). Justices Frankfurter and Stone dissented from the majority because they found that the Sherman Antitrust Act, the law that the companies were accused of violating, was not intended to be applied to the insurance industry.

[88] Codified at 15 U.S.C. § 1011 et seq.

[89] 15 U.S.C. § 1011.

[90] 15 U.S.C. § 1012 (b).

[91] 517 U.S. 25 (1996).

[92] P.L. 111-148, 124 Stat. 119.

[93] Codified at 26 U.S.C. § 5000A.

[94] NFIB v. Sebelius, 132 S. Ct. 603 (2011).

[95] NFIB, 132 S. Ct. at 2586-87.

[96] Id.

[97] For a detailed analysis of the Court's decision in this case, see CRS Report R42698, NFIB v. Sebelius: Constitutionality of the Individual Mandate, by Erika K. Lunder and Jennifer Staman.

[98] Specifically, P.L. 106-102, Title III, Subtitle C.

[99] 15 U.S.C. § 3901 et seq. For more information, see CRS Report RL32176, The Liability Risk Retention Act: Background, Issues, and Current Legislation, by Baird Webel.

[100] See U.S. Congress, House Committee on Financial Services, Subcommittee on Insurance, Housing and Community Opportunity, Insurance Oversight and Legislative Proposals, 112th Cong., 1st sess., November 16, 2011, http://financialservices.house.gov/calendar/eventsingle.aspx?EventID=268154.

[101] U.S. Treasury, "Treasury Releases Blueprint for Stronger Regulatory Structure," press release, March 31, 2008, available at http://www.ustreas.gov/press/releases/hp896.htm.

[102] See http://www.treasury.gov/initiatives/Documents/FinalReport_web.pdf.

In: Insurance Regulation: Background and Issues ISBN: 978-1-62948-141-8
Editor: Nelson R. Phillips

Chapter 2

INSURANCE AGENT LICENSING: OVERVIEW AND BACKGROUND ON FEDERAL "NARAB" LEGISLATION*

Baird Webel

SUMMARY

The individual states have been the primary regulators of insurance in this country for the past 150 years. Congress specifically authorized the states' role in the 1945 McCarran-Ferguson Act (15 U.S.C. §§1011-1015), and state primacy in insurance regulation has been recognized in more recent laws shaping the financial regulatory system, such as the 1999 Gramm-Leach-Bliley Act (GLBA; P.L. 106-102) and the 2010 Dodd-Frank Wall Street Reform and Consumer Protection Act (P.L. 111-203). The system of multiple state regulators, however, has faced criticism over the years, with frequent focus on the efficiency of the system. One particular aspect of regulation that has been criticized by some as overly burdensome and inefficient is the licensure of insurance agents and brokers, known collectively as insurance "producers." Every state requires specific licenses, sometimes with differing criteria, and insurance producers have identified the need to have multiple licenses as a significant expense for their operations.

---

* This is an edited, reformatted and augmented version of a Congressional Research Service publication, CRS Report for Congress R43095, prepared for Members and Committees of Congress, from www.crs.gov, dated July 1, 2013.

Organizations such as the National Association of Insurance Commissioners (NAIC) and the National Conference of Insurance Legislators (NCOIL) create model laws and undertake other steps to harmonize insurance regulation and laws across the country, including the promulgation by the NAIC of models for insurance producer licensing. The individual states, however, are sovereign entities, and any models suggested by the NAIC or NCOIL must first be enacted by state legislatures. The state authorities may amend models or may completely reject suggestions from outside groups. Often this is done with the argument that laws and regulations need to be adapted to particular local circumstances or risks, such as hurricane risks along coastal areas.

Federal proposals addressing multiple state insurance producer licensing requirements through the creation of a National Association of Registered Agents and Brokers (NARAB) appeared as far back as the 102nd Congress, and a version of NARAB was included in the Gramm-LeachBliley Act. These GLBA provisions, known generally as "NARAB I," were conditional, and would not come into effect if a majority of states passed laws providing for uniformity or reciprocity in insurance producer licensing. Although a sufficient number of states met the GLBA requirements and thereby prevented the creation of NARAB, insurance producers continued to identify issues in the state licensing system. As a consequence, "NARAB II" legislation, mandating the creation of a NARAB organization, was introduced in every Congress since the 110th. It was passed by the House in the 110th Congress and the 111th Congress, but was not considered by the Senate.

In the 113th Congress, the National Association of Registered Agents and Brokers Act of 2013 was introduced in both the Senate (S. 534) and the House (H.R. 1155). Under this legislation, membership in the NARAB organization to be created would permit insurance producers to operate in multiple states without obtaining specific licenses from these states. To become a NARAB member, an insurance producer would be required to have a license from at least one state, pass a criminal background check, and meet other requirements to be set by the association. The legislation would require that these additional requirements be not "less protective to the public" than the NAIC model law on insurance producer licensing. The association would be governed by a 13-member board made up of 8 current or former state insurance commissioners and 5 members from the insurance industry. The President would appoint the board, with advice and consent of the Senate, and retain the ability to remove the board and override the NARAB organization's rules or actions. S. 534 was amended and ordered favorably reported by the Senate Committee on Banking, Housing, and Urban Affairs on June 6, 2013.

INSURANCE REGULATION AND FEDERAL LEGISLATION

The individual states have been the primary regulators of insurance in this country for the past 150 years. The 1945 McCarran-Ferguson Act[1] specifically authorized the states' role, and Congress has recognized state primacy in insurance regulation in more recent laws shaping the financial regulatory system, such as 1999's Gramm-Leach-Bliley Act[2] (GLBA) and 2010's Dodd-Frank Wall Street Reform and Consumer Protection Act[3] (the Dodd-Frank Act). Although Congress may have generally reaffirmed the state-based system in such laws, congressional interest in the operation of the insurance regulatory system has continued.

Much of the congressional focus on the insurance regulatory system since 1999 has been on the efficiency of the state-based system. Organizations such as the National Association of Insurance Commissioners (NAIC) and the National Conference of Insurance Legislators (NCOIL) create model laws and undertake other steps to harmonize insurance regulation and laws across the country. To be legally binding, however, any models suggested by the NAIC or NCOIL must first be adopted in a state. The states may amend models to fit local circumstances or may completely reject suggestions from outside groups. Various federal proposals have been advanced to change the workings of the state-based regulatory system, ranging from creation of a broad federal charter that might replace much of the state-based system to narrower concepts using federal powers to preempt some state laws while leaving the state-based regulatory system largely in place.

In the 113th Congress, issues around licensing for insurance agents and brokers (known generally as "insurance producers") have come to the fore in the form of legislation—the National Association of Registered Agents and Brokers Act of 2013, introduced in both the Senate (S. 534) and the House (H.R. 1155/H.R. 1064). This legislation, which would *mandate* the creation of a National Association of Registered Agents and Brokers (NARAB), is generally referred to as "NARAB II" legislation. "NARAB I" generally refers to provisions included in the GrammLeach-Bliley Act,[4] which *conditionally* allowed for the creation of a NARAB, but never took effect. Legislative language creating some version of a NARAB predated GLBA and appeared as part of broader legislation in the House during the 102nd and 103rd Congresses; this legislation was referred to committee and subcommittee hearings were held, but it did not advance further in the legislative process.

INSURANCE PRODUCER LICENSING

Licensing of insurance agents and brokers (known generally as "insurance producers") has long been an integral part of the insurance regulatory system. Individual states typically require insurance producers operating within their borders to obtain a license from that state with different licenses required often for different lines of insurance. Such licensure provides a mechanism for insurance regulators to enforce standards of conduct, particularly with regard to consumer protections, as well as provides a revenue source to help defray the cost of the insurance regulatory system. Aspects of insurance producer licensing include specific education or knowledge requirements, such as passage of a written exam prior to licensing and continuing education afterwards and, in some states, criminal background checks.

The NAIC has adopted model laws regarding licensure and a model insurance producer license form, but individual states are free to modify such models, or not adopt them at all, resulting in variability in licensing requirements across the country. The number of insurance producers potentially affected by the variability of state licensing laws appears relatively large; in one survey, 83% of producers reported having licenses in at least 2 and up to 10 states. Larger insurance agencies tend to hold a larger number of licenses, with 47% of the firms of more than 500 financial advisors having licenses in 21 or more states.[5] Insurance producers who operate in multiple states have long sought increased uniformity and reciprocity across states to reduce their costs resulting from the multiplicity of license requirements. Insurance producers report, for example, that, on average, 3% of agency operating expenses are spent on "licensing compliance efforts," with higher figures (4.3%) at the smallest agencies.[6] Although insurance producers consider the multiplicity of licenses to be a burden, the requirements for local licenses and knowledge of specific local risks or legal requirements are considered important consumer protections by others. One consumer representative has argued, for example, "[Property and casualty] insurance varies too much state to state as respects law and risk to not maintain local control of licensure."[7]

The Gramm-Leach-Bliley Act attempted to address the multiplicity of different requirements among states for insurance producer licensing. Although many states satisfied the GLBA statutory requirements for reciprocity by 2002, insurance producers continued to identify inefficiencies and costs of the state licensing system in the years following. In 2008 testimony before a House subcommittee, for example, an insurance agent representative indicated that states continued to "impose additional conditions and requirements"[8] on non-resident agents despite the reciprocity called for in law. In 2009, the Government Accountability Office (GAO) cited issues regarding fingerprinting and background checks as particular barriers to uniformity or reciprocity in producer licensing and as potentially creating uneven insurance consumer protection in states where full-background checks were not able to be performed. GAO also found differences in licensing requirements and insurance line definitions as potentially creating inefficiencies that "could result in higher costs for insurers, which in turn could be passed on to consumer[s]."[9] In addition to concerns about the substance of the reciprocity in place, reciprocity laws have not been adopted by every state. The NAIC ultimately certified 47 states as reciprocal, but the 3 states not certified were California, Florida, and Washington, which together represented nearly 20% of the nation's population.

In addition to the costs that might result from the specific aspects of the insurance licensing system, any professional licensing regime acts as a barrier to entry for those who might be interested in providing services that require a license. Economic theory suggests that such barriers increase consumer costs to some degree and have the potential to be used as a protectionist measure to prevent competition, allowing license-holders to extract economic rents from consumers. Whether the public benefits resulting from licensure outweigh the costs is determined by policymakers on a case-by-case basis. Some form of licensure for those in the financial services industry has been generally accepted and is required in federal law for people involved in securities transactions with the public, for example.

LEGISLATION IN THE 113TH CONGRESS

The National Association of Registered Agents and Brokers Reform Act of 2013 (S. 534 and H.R. 1155)

The National Association of Registered Agents and Brokers Reform Act of 2013, S. 534, was introduced in the Senate by Senator Jon Tester on March 13, 2013, and referred to the Senate Committee on Banking, Housing, and Urban Affairs. The committee's Subcommittee on Securities, Insurance, and Investment held a hearing on the bill on March 19, 2013,[10] and the full committee marked up S. 534 and ordered the amended bill be favorably reported on June 6, 2013.

Representative Randy Neugebauer introduced an identical bill as H.R. 1155 on March 14, 2013, and it was referred to the House Committee on Financial Services.[11]

S. 534 and H.R. 1155 as introduced would establish a National Association of Registered Agents and Brokers. Key features of this association include the following:

- The association would be a private, nonprofit corporation.
- To gain membership, insurance producers would be required to be licensed as an insurance producer in their home state, pass a criminal background check, and meet other criteria determined by the association, which shall not be "less protective of the public than that contained in the NAIC Producer Licensing Model Act."[12]
- NARAB members would be able to operate in any other state subject only to payment of the licensing fee in that state, rather than having to obtain a separate license in the additional states, as is often the case now.
- Members would still be subject to each state's consumer protection and market conduct regulation, but individual state laws that treat out-of-state insurance producers differently from in-state producers would be preempted.
- The association would be overseen by a board made up of eight appointees who are current or former state insurance commissioners and five appointees representing the insurance industry. The appointments would be made by the President with advice and consent by the Senate.
- The President could dissolve the board as a whole or suspend the implementation of any rule or action taken by the association.
- The association would submit annual reports to the President and the National Association of Insurance Commissioners.

Senate Committee Consideration

The Senate Committee on Banking, Housing, and Urban Affairs marked up S. 534 on June 6, 2013. The committee began with an amendment in the nature of a substitute offered by Senators Jon Tester and Mike Johanns. Although largely similar to the original legislation, this amendment made changes to the bill, including

- adding the Department of the Treasury as a conduit of information from NARAB to the President;
- requiring that copies of the NARAB bylaws, standards, and annual report be publically available on the NARAB website; and
- requiring the annual report be made to the President and the "States (including the State insurance regulators)" rather than the President and the NAIC (the NAIC was also removed from some, but not all, of the other reporting requirements in the bill).

In addition to the substitute, four amendments were offered in the markup. An amendment by Senator Tom Coburn to provide states the ability to opt out of participation in, and the effect of, NARAB was not adopted on a vote of 18-4. An amendment regarding the National Flood Insurance Program was offered by Senator David Vitter, but was withdrawn prior to a vote. Two amendments were adopted by voice vote. These amendments changed the following:

- The board of directors would have five appointees with "demonstrated expertise and experience" in various parts of the insurance industry, rather than being "representatives of" various parts of the industry following an amendment by Senator Elizabeth Warren.
- The NARAB organization would be specifically forbidden from receiving federal funds following an amendment by Senator Tom Coburn.

The amended version of S. 534 was ordered to be favorably reported by voice vote.

PAST NARAB LEGISLATION

NARAB II

Legislation to *mandate* the creation of a NARAB organization, similar to S. 534 and H.R. 1155/H.R. 1064, was first introduced into the House of Representatives in the 110th Congress (H.R. 5611), with similar legislation introduced in the 111th Congress (H.R. 2554). The House passed these bills in the respective Congresses by voice vote, and the legislation was referred to committee when received by the Senate. NARAB II legislation was introduced in the 112th Congress (H.R. 1112 and S. 2342), but, unlike the previous Congresses, the House did not bring NARAB legislation to the floor in the 112th Congress.

The general outlines of the various NARAB II bills have remained similar. The various bills would amend the NARAB sections to create a NARAB organization regardless of state actions on reciprocity and uniformity. NARAB II legislation would create an organization similar to that originally envisioned in GLBA. It would be a nonprofit, private body, whose members would be required to be state-licensed insurance producers, but who could operate across states without having licenses from the individual states. The specifics of the NARAB II bills have, however, differed to some degree, particularly in the makeup of the board of directors and how the board would be appointed. The initial NARAB II legislation (H.R. 5611, 110th Congress) included a nine-person board of directors, four to be appointed by the NAIC and five to be appointed by the insurance industry. This was changed to an 11-person (6 insurance commissioners/5 insurance industry representatives) board to be appointed by the President with Senate confirmation in H.R. 2554 (111th Congress) and H.R. 1112 (112th Congress). The NARAB board was then changed to be a 13-person (8 insurance commissioners/5 insurance industry representatives) presidentially appointed and Senate-confirmed board in S. 2342 (112th Congress) and the current legislation. In addition, H.R. 5611 required a report by the NARAB association to the President, Congress, and the NAIC, while subsequent legislation required the report be made solely to the President and the NAIC.[13]

NARAB I

Legislative provisions creating a "National Association of Registered Agents and Brokers" appeared as part of broad financial regulatory reform legislation in the 105th Congress[14] and the 106th Congress,[15] ultimately becoming law as part of what is generally known as the GrammLeach-Bliley Act in the 106th Congress. GLBA sought to address insurance producer complaints about the variation in state licensing requirements through a sort of provisional federal preemption of state laws. The law called for the creation of a private, nonprofit licensing body, the National Association of Registered Agents and Brokers, whose insurance producer members would have been authorized to operate across state lines without individual licenses from every state. Membership in NARAB I would have been open only to people already holding a state insurance producer license and who fulfilled other criteria. Although established by federal authority, the NARAB to be created by the provisions in GLBA would have been entwined in the system of state regulation. The NAIC would have appointed the seven members of the NARAB I board and had other oversight authorities.

The NARAB I language in GLBA also offered the states the opportunity to avoid creation of the NARAB I organization if a majority of the states created among themselves systems of either uniformity or reciprocity in insurance producer licensing within a three-year window after passage of GLBA. The NAIC was given the authority to determine whether the states met this GLBA standard, with the possibility of federal judicial review of the determination. The individual states and the NAIC reacted relatively quickly to this opportunity with the promulgation of an NAIC model law that would provide for reciprocity. A sufficient number of states adopted laws providing for insurance producer licensing reciprocity that the NAIC determined the GLBA standards to avoid creation of the NARAB I organization were met. As a result, the NARAB I organization was not created.

Original NARAB Provisions

The first legislation specifically providing for the creation of a "National Association of Registered Agents and Brokers" that the Congressional Research Service has been able to identify was introduced in the 102nd Congress (Title IV of H.R. 4900).[16] The bill was reintroduced in the 103rd Congress[17] and subcommittee hearings were held that addressed NARAB,[18] but the bill was not acted on further.

The original NARAB provisions were part of legislation that would have created a federal commission for solvency oversight of insurers. The NARAB created by this legislation would have been similar to subsequent versions in that it would have been a nonprofit association whose members would have been state-licensed insurance producers, but the preemption of state law would have been narrower than in subsequent versions. The original version of NARAB would not have permitted its members to operate with a single state license, but instead would have operated to enforce uniformity though a central clearinghouse and a uniform producer application. The board of directors would have been elected by the membership, and the Federal

Solvency Commission to be created by the bill would have had oversight authority over this version of NARAB.

End Notes

[1] 15 U.S.C. §§1011-1015.

[2] P.L. 106-102.

[3] P.L. 111-203.

[4] Specifically, P.L. 106-102, Title III, Subtitle C.

[5] Survey statistics provided to CRS by the Insured Retirement Institute.

[6] Statement of Jon Jensen on Behalf of The Independent Insurance Agents & Brokers of America, before U.S. Congress, Senate Committee on Banking, Housing, and Urban Affairs, Subcommittee on Securities, Insurance, and Investment, Streamlining Regulation, Improving Consumer Protection and Increasing Competition in Insurance Markets, Hearing on S. 534, 113th Cong., 1st sess., March 19, 2013, p. 2, available at http://www.banking.senate.gov/ public/index.cfm?FuseAction=Files.View&FileStore_id=446f26f8-226d-436f-9894-8fe387828128.

[7] J. Robert Hunter, Insurance Director, Consumer Federation of America, quoted in NCOILLETTER, Issue 3, 2013, p.3, available at http://www.ncoil.org/news/ 2013_newsletters/Vol32013.pdf.

[8] Statement of Tom Minkler on behalf of the Independent Insurance Agents & Brokers Of America, before U.S. Congress, House Committee Financial Services, Subcommittee on Capital Markets, Insurance, and Government Sponsored Enterprises, Examining Proposals on Insurance Regulatory Reform, 110th Cong., 2nd sess., April 16, 2008, p. 6, available at http://archives.financialservices.house.gov/hearing110/minkler041608.pdf.

[9] U.S. Government Accountability Office, Insurance Reciprocity and Uniformity, GAO-09-372, April 6, 2009, p. 21, available at http://www.gao.gov/products/GAO-09-372.

[10] U.S. Congress, Senate Committee on Banking, Housing, and Urban Affairs, Subcommittee on Securities, Insurance, and Investment, Streamlining Regulation, Improving Consumer Protection and Increasing Competition in Insurance Markets, Hearing on S. 534, 113th Cong., 1st sess., March 19, 2013. Hearing webcast and statements can be found at http://www.banking.senate.gov/public/index.cfm?FuseAction=Hearings.Hearing&Hearing_ID=72d49be4-ff44-4d01- 862a-4654e13b2589.

[11] A previous version of this bill was introduced by Representative Neugebauer as H.R. 1064. However, the Committee on Financial Services staff has indicated to CRS that H.R. 1155 will be used as the legislative vehicle going forward, so this report will concentrate on this bill.

[12] §323(d)(2) of S. 534 as introduced in the 113th Congress.

[13] The U.S. Department of Justice sent a letter to the Senate leadership following House passage of H.R. 5611 that identified concerns with the bill, including the appointments language in the bill and the requirement for reporting to Congress. See http://www.justice.gov/archive/ola/views-letters/110-2/10-01-08-hr5611-agents-brokers-reform-act.pdf.

[14] Title IV of H.R. 10 and Title III, Subtitle B of S. 2590.

[15] Title IV of H.R. 10 and Title III, Subtitle C of S. 900.

[16] The Federal Insurance Solvency Act of 1992 (H.R. 4900), introduced by Rep. John Dingell on May 8, 1992.

[17] The Federal Insurance Solvency Act of 1993 (H.R. 1290), introduced by Rep. John Dingell on March 10, 1993.

[18] U.S. Congress, House Committee on Energy and Commerce, Subcommittee on Commerce, Consumer Protection, and Competitiveness, Federal Insurance Solvency, hearing on H.R. 1290, 103rd Cong., 1st sess., April 28, 1993, 103-40, pp. 385-458.

In: Insurance Regulation: Background and Issues ISBN: 978-1-62948-141-8
Editor: Nelson R. Phillips

Chapter 3

INSURANCE REGULATION: FEDERAL CHARTER LEGISLATION*

Baird Webel

SUMMARY

Insurance is one of three primary sectors of the financial services industry. Unlike the other two, banks and securities, insurance is primarily regulated at the state, rather than federal, level. The primacy of state regulation dates back to 1868 when the Supreme Court found in Paul v. Virginia (75 U.S. (8 Wall.) 168 (1868)) that insurance did not constitute interstate commerce, and thus did not fall under the powers granted the federal government in the Constitution. In 1944, however, the Court cast doubt on this finding in United States v. South-Eastern Underwriters Association (322 U.S. 533 (1944)). Preferring to leave the state regulatory system intact in the aftermath of this decision, Congress passed the McCarran-Ferguson Act of 1945 (P.L. 79-15, 59 Stat. 33), which reaffirmed the states as principal regulators of insurance. Over the years since 1945, congressional interest in the possibility of repealing McCarran-Ferguson and reclaiming authority over insurance regulation has waxed and waned.

Particularly since the Gramm-Leach-Bliley Act of 1999 (P.L. 106-102, 113 Stat. 1338), the financial services industry has seen increased

* This is an edited, reformatted and augmented version of a Congressional Research Service publication, CRS Report for Congress RL34286, prepared for Members and Committees of Congress, from www.crs.gov, dated February 3, 2011.

competition among U.S. banks, insurers, and securities firms and on a global scale. Some have complained that the state regulatory system puts insurers at a competitive disadvantage. Whereas the insurance industry had previously been united in preferring the state system, it has now splintered, with larger insurers tending to argue for a federal system and smaller insurers tending to favor the state system.

Some members of Congress have responded with different proposals ranging from a complete federalization of the interstate insurance industry, to leaving the state system intact with limited federal standards and preemptions.

A common proposal in the past has been for an Optional Federal Charter (OFC) for the insurance industry. This idea borrows the idea of a dual regulatory system from the banking system. Both the states and the federal government would offer a chartering system for insurers, with the insurers having the choice between the two. OFC legislation was offered in the 107th, 109th, and 110th Congresses.

Proponents of OFC legislation typically have cited the efficiencies that could be gained from a uniform system, along with the ability of a federal regulator to better address the complexities of the current insurance market and ongoing financial crisis as well as the need for a single federal voice for the insurance industry in international negotiations.

Opponents of OFC legislation have been typically concerned with the inability of a federal regulator to take into account local conditions, the lack of consumer service that could result from a nonlocal administrator in Washington, DC, and the overall deregulation contained in some of the OFC proposals.

The recent financial crisis gave greater urgency to calls for federal oversight of insurance and has changed the tenor of the debate. The National Insurance Consumer Protection Act of 2009 (H.R. 1880) was introduced in the 111th Congress by two previous sponsors of OFC legislation. This bill differed significantly from previous OFC bills as it included the creation of a new systemic risk regulator with the power to mandate the adoption of a federal charter by some insurers. The broad Dodd-Frank Act (P.L. 111-203) that was enacted to reform the financial system included some insurance aspects, but did not include a federal charter for insurance. Such legislation has not been introduced in the 112th Congress.

This report offers a brief analysis of the forces prompting federal chartering legislation, followed by a discussion of the arguments for and against a federal charter, and summaries of previous legislation.

BACKGROUND

Insurance is one of three primary sectors of the financial services industry. Unlike the other two, banks and securities, insurance is primarily regulated at the state, rather than federal, level. The primacy of state regulation dates back to 1868 when the Supreme Court found that insurance did not constitute interstate commerce, and thus did not fall under the powers granted the federal government in the Constitution.[1] In 1944, however, the Court cast doubt on this finding.[2] Preferring to leave the state regulatory system intact in the aftermath of this decision, Congress passed the McCarran-Ferguson Act of 1945,[3] which reaffirmed the states as principal regulators of insurance. Over the years since 1945, congressional interest in the possibility of repealing or amending McCarran-Ferguson and reclaiming authority over insurance regulation has waxed and waned.

In 1974, Congress passed the Employee Retirement Income Security Act[4] (ERISA) preempting state laws governing many health benefit plans offered by employers, thus essentially federalizing much of the regulation of health insurance. In 1980, Congress curtailed the authority of the Federal Trade Commission (FTC) to investigate the insurance industry, reducing a small avenue of federal oversight on insurance.[5] In the early 1990s, a bill[6] to repeal the limited antitrust exemption granted insurers in McCarran-Ferguson, and thus expand federal oversight of insurance, was reported out of committee in the House, but never reached the House floor. In 1999, Congress passed the Gramm-Leach-Bliley Act[7] (GLBA), which specifically reaffirmed the states as the functional regulators of insurance.

GLBA may have statutorily reaffirmed the primacy of state regulation of insurance, but it also unleashed market forces that were already encouraging a greater federal role. GLBA removed legal barriers between securities firms, banks, and insurers, which, along with improved technology, have been an important factor in creating more direct competition among the three groups. Many financial products have converged, so that products with similar economic outcomes may be available from different financial services firms with dramatically different regulators. Insurers face 50 different state regulators and state laws, many of which differ on some particulars of insurance regulation. This has led to industry complaints of overlapping, and sometimes contradictory, regulatory edicts driving up the cost of compliance and increasing the time necessary to bring new products to market. These complaints existed prior to GLBA, but the insurance industry generally resisted federalization of insurance regulation at the time. Facing a new world of competition, however, the industry split, with larger insurers tending to favor some form of federal regulation, and smaller insurers tending to favor a continuation of the state regulatory system. Life insurers tend to more directly compete with banks and securities firms, so they have tended to favor some form of federal charter more than property/casualty insurers.

Some members of Congress have responded to the changing environment in the financial services industry with a variety of legislation. In the 108th Congress, Senator Ernest Hollings introduced S. 1373 to create a mandatory federal charter for insurance. In the 108th and 109th Congresses, Representative Richard Baker drafted, but never introduced, the SMART Act[8] that would have left the states the primary regulators, but harmonized the system through various federal preemptions. The most consistent response has been the introduction of legislation calling for an Optional Federal Charter (OFC) for insurance.

OFC legislation was first introduced in the 107th Congress, with bills being introduced in the 109th and 110th Congresses as well. Specifics of OFC legislation can vary widely, but the common thread is the creation of a dual regulatory system, inspired by the current banking regulatory system. OFC bills generally would create a federal insurance regulator that would operate concurrently with the present state system. Insurers would be able to choose whether to take out a federal charter, which would exempt them from most state insurance regulations, or to continue under a state charter and the 50 state system of insurance regulation. Given the greater uniformity of life insurance products and the greater competition faced by life insurers, some have suggested the possibility of OFC legislation that would apply only to life insurers, but no such bills have been introduced.

The recent financial crisis affected the debate over federal chartering for insurers in a variety of ways. Some aspects of the crisis gave additional arguments for federal chartering, whereas other aspects have given additional arguments against federal chartering. One specific concern that many have advanced in the crisis has been the negative aspects of allowing financial institutions to choose their regulators. The broad federal charter bill in the 111th Congress, H.R. 1880, addressed this by adding some mandatory aspects to a framework similar to the previous OFC bills.

During the December 2, 2009, House Financial Services Committee markup of H.R. 2609, a bill to create a Federal Office of Insurance, two amendments were offered to create federal licenses and regulation of specific lines of insurance. Representative Dennis Moore offered an amendment (no. 3) that would have created an optional federal license for reinsurers, while

Representatives Ed Royce and Melissa Bean offered an amendment (no. 7) that would have created an optional federal license for financial guarantee insurers.[9] Both were withdrawn before votes were taken on the amendments. H.R. 2609 was incorporated into H.R. 4173, which was ultimately enacted as the Dodd-Frank Act[10] and included some insurance provisions, but did not include a federal charter for insurance.[11] Representative Moore introduced his amendment creating a federal license for reinsurers as a standalone bill, H.R. 6529, on December 16, 2010.

The Debate on Federal Chartering for Insurers

Many different arguments have been advanced for and against a dual regulatory system for insurance. While taking no position in this debate, many of these arguments are listed below.

Arguments for a Dual Regulatory System

In addition to the principal argument that the regulation of insurance companies needs to be overhauled at the federal level to enable insurers to become more competitive with other federally regulated financial institutions in the post-GLBA environment, other arguments advanced for dual chartering have included the following:

- The recent financial crisis has shown that some insurers can present systemic risk and therefore should be regulated by a regulator with a broader outlook.
- A federal insurance regulator could be a knowledgeable voice and an insurance advocate in Washington, DC. (The Dodd-Frank Act addressed this to some degree through the creation of a "Federal Insurance Office," though this office has no regulatory powers.)
- The Comptroller of the Currency has successfully promoted the expansion of bank products through preemption of state laws, providing a model for the insurance sector.
- The increase of "speed to market" for product approval so insurers will not be at a disadvantage in product creation and delivery.
- The creation of a regulatory environment more accommodating of growth and innovation as a result of competition between federal and state regulators.

- The ability to achieve national treatment, so that a single charter would allow insurers to do business in all states and avoid higher costs of state regulation due to the need to comply with up to 50 state regulators.
- Potential difficulty insurers face in international trade without a regulator at the national level.
- Greater supply of insurance and lower cost to consumers as insurance companies are forced to compete on a national scale.

Arguments Against a Dual System and for State Regulation

The arguments of those who oppose federal regulation of insurance companies, preferring that the state insurance regulatory system be maintained, have included the following:

- State regulated insurers have performed relatively well through the financial crisis, underscoring the quality of state regulation.
- State insurance regulators have a better understanding of local markets and conditions that would a federal regulator.
- State regulation is more flexible and adaptable to local conditions.
- The diversity of state regulation reduces the impact of any poor regulation and promotes innovation and good regulation.
- There are strong incentives, such as those provided by direct election, for state regulators to do the job effectively at the state level.
- The risk that the new federal bureaucracy would end up being redundant and costly.
- Fiscal damage to the states should state premium taxes be reduced by a federal system.[12]
- The fragmentation of the overall insurance regulatory system that could result from dual chartering and state/federal oversight.
- The possibility of a "race to the bottom" as state and federal regulators compete to give insurers more favorable treatment and thus secure greater oversight authority and budget.

In the abstract, the federal chartering question could be simply about the "who" of regulation. Should it be the federal government, the states, or some combination of the two? In practice, however, federal chartering legislation has had much to say about the "how" of regulation. Should the government continue the same fine degree of industry oversight that states have practiced in the past? Aside from Senator Hollings' bill in the 108th Congress, the federal chartering bills that have been introduced to this point have tended to answer the latter question negatively—the federal regulator to be created would exercise less regulatory oversight than would most state regulators. This deregulatory aspect of past bills has been source of controversy in addition to the introduction of federal regulation itself.

PREVIOUS FEDERAL CHARTERING LEGISLATION

111th Congress

The National Insurance Consumer Protection Act (H.R. 1880)

Representatives Melissa Bean and Edward Royce introduced H.R. 1880 in the House on April 2, 2009. The bill was referred to the House Financial Services Committee, House Judiciary Committee, and House Energy and Commerce Committee. No hearings or markups were held on this bill.

H.R. 1880 would have created a federal chartering and regulatory apparatus for the insurance industry, including insurers, insurance agencies, and independent insurance producers. The Office of National Insurance (ONI) and a National Insurance Commissioner (NIC) would have been established in the Department of the Treasury, but with significant independence; the Secretary of the Treasury would have been forbidden from interfering in specific matters before the commissioner; the ONI's budget would have been funded by fees and assessments on insurers; and the commissioner would have been appointed by the President, and confirmed by the Senate for a five-year term. These terms are similar to those of other financial regulators, such as the Office of the Comptroller of the Currency.

The federal regulatory system in H.R. 1880 would have applied to property/casualty and life insurance and reinsurance, with the exception of title insurance. Federally licensed insurance producers were specifically allowed to sell surplus lines insurance. [13] Holders of a national charter or license would have been exempt from most state insurance laws, including "any form of licensing, examination, reporting, regulation, or supervision by a State relating to the insurance operations of such insurer."[14] Thus, nationally licensed insurers, agencies, and producers would have been able to operate in the entire United States without fulfilling the requirements of the 50 states' insurance laws. This exemption, however, did not extend to state premium tax laws, so national insurers would have continued to pay these taxes. The bill would have affected state taxes with regard to surplus lines insurance, forbidding states that are not the home state of the insured from collecting these taxes.

In terms of the substance of regulation, the most significant specific change in H.R. 1880 compared with the way most states currently regulate insurance involves regulation of insurance rates and forms. Currently every state has some measure of rate and form regulation.[15] In some states, insurers must get specific prior approval for changes to rates and forms, whereas in others insurers may have some freedom to change rates and forms with the possibility that the state insurance commissioner could disallow the change after the fact. This bill, however, would have specifically disallowed the NIC from regulating insurance rates. With regard to form regulation, the commissioner would have had the power to set general form requirements and insurers would have been required to file insurance forms with the commissioner along with a certification that the forms met the established requirements.

H.R. 1880 would have specifically addressed the issue of systemic risk brought to the fore in the recent financial crisis in two ways. It would have required that a financial regulator other than the ONI be designated a systemic risk regulator for insurance with power over both national insurers and state insurers. This regulator would have had broad oversight powers, including the ability, in consultation with the NIC, to require an insurer be federally chartered. H.R. 1880 would also have created a "Coordinating National Council for Financial Regulators" made up of the heads of the various federal financial regulators along with the Secretary of the Treasury. This council would have been responsible for monitoring the financial system for systemic risk with the specific power to determine when the systemic risk regulator could issue a rule or direct order covering an insurer that presented systemic risk.

H.R. 1880 shared many aspects with previous optional federal chartering bills, including legislation introduced by Representatives Bean and Royce. Under H.R. 1880, many insurers would have had the option to choose whether to operate under a federal or state system. The system to be put in place by the bill, however, has two specific non-optional aspects: (1) The NIC had the specific authority to deny an application from a national insurer to convert to a state charter; and (2) the systemic risk regulator had the specific authority to require an insurer to become federally chartered.

The Federal License for Reinsurers Act of 2010 (H.R. 6529)

Representative Dennis Moore introduced H.R. 6529 on December 16, 2010. It was referred to the House Committee on Financial Services but no hearings or markups were held on the bill. H.R. 6529 would have created a federal license for reinsurers. The licensing and regulatory authority would rest with the Federal Insurance Office, which was created under the Dodd-Frank Act, which would have the authority to determine that state laws were inconsistent with federal law and thus preempted.

110th Congress

The National Insurance Act of 2007 (S. 40/H.R. 3200)

Senators John Sununu and Tim Johnson introduced S. 40 on May 24, 2007 and Representatives Melissa Bean and Edward Royce introduced H.R. 3200 on July 26, 2007. The bills were referred to the relevant committees (Senate Banking, Housing, and Urban Affairs, House Financial Services, and House Judiciary), but neither was the specific subject of hearings or markups. Two general hearings on insurance regulatory reform, however, were held by the House Financial Services Subcommittee on Capital Markets, Insurance, and Government Sponsored Enterprises in October 2007, and the possibility of an optional federal charter was a major topic of discussion in the subcommittee.

S. 40 and H.R. 3200 were very similar, but not identical bills. Both would have created the option of a federal charter for the insurance industry, including insurers, insurance agencies, and independent insurance producers. The bills would have created a federal regulatory and supervisory apparatus, including an Office of National Insurance and a National Insurance Commissioner. This federal regulator would generally have been overseen by the Secretary of the Treasury, but the secretary would have been forbidden from interfering in specific matters before the commissioner. The budget for the office would have been paid for by fees and assessments on insurers. The commissioner would have been appointed by the President, and confirmed by the Senate for a five-year term. Holders of a national license would have been exempt from most state insurance laws. Thus, nationally licensed insurers, agencies, and producers would have been able to operate in the entire United States without fulfilling the requirements of the 50 states' insurance laws. Some significant aspects of the bills included the following:

- The federal system would have applied to property/casualty and life insurance, except for title insurance and including surplus lines insurance.[16]
- Rate regulation would not have been applicable to national insurers.
- Form regulation, the ability of the regulator to control what will and will not be included in an insurance policy, would have been reduced substantially compared with most states.
- Fees covering the cost of the system would have been assessed on those operating under the federal system.
- National insurers would have continued to pay state premium taxes, so there should be no loss of premium tax revenue to the states.
- National insurers would have continued to be subject to state laws requiring participation in residual market entities, but only if rates charged by the residual market entity covers all costs incurred, and only if there were no rate and form requirements concurrent with participation.
- Reform of the state regulation of surplus lines insurance—only the state in which the insured resides or does business would be allowed to tax surplus lines insurance.
- National insurance producers would have been allowed to sell surplus lines insurance.
- Would have applied federal antitrust laws to national insurers, except to the extent that state laws continue to apply to them.

Differences between S. 40 and H.R. 3200 are relatively minor, including the following:

- H.R. 3200 would have specifically allowed non-U.S. reinsurers to file financial data in accordance with International Financial Reporting Standards.
- H.R. 3200 would have limited jurisdiction over non-U.S. reinsurers to federal courts, rather than including state and local courts.
- H.R. 3200 would have broadened slightly and clarify antifraud language.

Beyond the general aspects inherent in the OFC concept, such as the dual, competing regulatory structures and uniform regulation across the country, the most striking specific aspect of S. 40 and H.R. 3200 was the lessening of the rate and form regulation under these bills as compared to the current system. Currently every state has some measure of rate and form regulation.[17] In some states, insurers must get specific prior approval for changes to rates and forms, while in others insurers may have some freedom to change rates and forms with the possibility that the state insurance commissioner could disallow the change after the fact. S. 40 and H.R. 3200 specifically disallowed rate and form regulation for national property/casualty insurers. Such insurers would have been required only to maintain copies of the policy forms that they use. National life insurers would have been subject to general standards and a requirement to file forms with the commissioner before these forms would have been used.

109th Congress

The National Insurance Act of 2006 (S. 2509/H.R. 6225)

Senators John Sununu and Tim Johnson introduced S. 2509 on April 5, 2006. The House companion, H.R. 6225 was introduced on October 18, 2006. Neither bill saw direct committee action, although S. 2509 was repeatedly discussed at a hearing on "Perspectives in Insurance Regulation," held by the Senate Banking, Housing, and Urban Affairs Committee on July 18, 2006. These bills were very similar to the bills of the same name introduced in the 110th Congress and discussed above. Differences between the bills in the two Congresses included the following:

- The 2006 bills did not address surplus lines insurance.
- The 2007 bills added language requiring national insurer compliance with anti-money laundering laws.
- The 2007 bills specifically exclude national insurers from offering title insurance.
- The 2007 bills included new guaranty fund language, changing the focus from a qualified state, to a qualified association or fund. If a state's guaranty fund is not qualified, then the national insurers operating in that state must join the national guaranty fund to be established by the NIC.

108th Congress

Insurance Consumer Protection Act of 2003 (S. 1373)

On July 8, 2003, Senator Ernest Hollings introduced S. 1373, "A bill to authorize and direct the Secretary of Commerce, through an independent commission within the Department of Commerce, to protect consumers by regulating the interstate sale of insurance, and for other purposes." The bill was referred to the Senate Commerce, Science, and Transportation Committee, where it was discussed in a general hearing on insurance regulation but was not acted upon further. Senator Hollings retired following the 108th Congress.

S. 1373 would have created a mandatory federal charter for interstate property/casualty and life insurers, leaving only single state insurers to be regulated by the state where they were domiciled and operated. It thus would have preempted most current state regulation of insurance. Significant aspects of the bill included the following:

- Creation of a federal commission within the Department of Commerce to regulate the interstate business of property/casualty and life insurance.
- Grant of full regulatory powers to the commission, including licensure, rate and form approval, regulation of solvency, and regulation of market conduct.
- Repeal of the antitrust exemptions in the McCarran-Ferguson Act.
- Creation of a federal guaranty fund.

107th Congress

The Insurance Industry Modernization and Consumer Protection Act (H.R. 3766)

H.R. 3766 was introduced on February 14, 2002, by Representative John LaFalce. It would have created an optional federal charter for "national insurers," but not for insurance agencies, brokers, or agents. It would have created a new federal agency within the Treasury Department, known as the Office of National Insurers and headed by a director, rather than a commissioner. Other significant aspects of H.R. 3766 included the following:

- The federal charter would have provided for a national insurer to underwrite both life insurance and property/casualty insurance.
- The director would have had general regulatory authority over national insurers, including solvency oversight and policy forms, but rate regulation would have been left with state insurance regulators.
- Even though the legislation had no provision for the licensing of insurance producers, the director would have had the authority to enforce unfair and deceptive practices rules against state-licensed producers with respect to the sale of insurance products issued by national insurers, and all states would have been subject to federal minimum standards.
- National insurers would have been encouraged to invest in the communities in which they sell policies.
- National insurers would have been required to file reports containing community sales data for use by federal regulators in combating insurance redlining. Further, national insurers would have been prohibited from refusing to insure, or limiting coverage on a property, based solely on its geographic location.

The National Insurance Chartering and Supervision Act

This proposal was reportedly introduced late in 2001 by Senator Charles Schumer, but was never assigned a number, nor referred to either the Senate Commerce Committee or the Senate Banking, Housing, and Urban Affairs Committee.[18] A draft of this proposal[19] provided that the chartering, supervision, and regulation of National Insurance Companies and National Insurance Agencies be administered by the federal government in a newly created federal agency within the Treasury Department. The proposed agency, the Office of the National Insurance Commissioner, would have been headed by the NIC, appointed for a five-year term by the President and subject to Senate confirmation. National insurers and agents would have been exempt from most state insurance law. Significant aspects of the bill included the following:

- application to all lines of insurance, including life, health, and property/casualty;
- imposition of fees as necessary to cover the expenses of the federal apparatus; and

- requirement that NICs participate in "qualified" state insurance guaranty associations and establishment of a federal backup guaranty association to cover "non-qualifying" states.

The broad powers granted to the NIC were not to include the authority to regulate rates or policy forms. Nor would the Schumer proposal have exempted federally chartered NICs from antitrust laws, except for purposes of preparing policy forms and participating in state residual market programs such as assigned risk pools in automobile insurance. The federal license would have specified the line or lines of insurance a NIC could underwrite, and no single NIC could be licensed to underwrite both life/health insurance and property/casualty insurance, although an affiliated group of insurance companies (state and/or federally chartered) could have included separate companies writing those different lines of insurance.

End Notes

[1] Paul v. Virginia (75 U.S. (8 Wall.) 168 (1868)).
[2] United States v. South-Eastern Underwriters Association (322 U.S. 533 (1944)).
[3] P.L. 79-15, 59 Stat. 33,15 U.S.C. Sec. 1011 et seq.
[4] P.L. 93-406, 88 Stat. 829.
[5] The Federal Trade Commission Improvement Act of 1980, P.L. 96-252, 94 Stat. 374.
[6] H.R. 9, The Insurance Competitive Pricing Act of 1994, by Representative Jack Brooks.
[7] P.L. 106-102, 113 Stat. 1338.
[8] This act was the subject of a June 16, 2005, hearing in the House Financial Services Subcommittee on Capital Markets, Insurance, and Government Sponsored Enterprises entitled "SMART Insurance Reform."
[9] Information on the markup, including amendment texts, can be found on the House Financial Services Committee website at http://www.house.gov/apps/list/speech/financialsvcs_dem/Mrkp_110309.shtml.
[10] P.L. 111-203.
[11] See CRS Report R41372, The Dodd-Frank Wall Street Reform and Consumer Protection Act: Insurance Provisions, by Baird Webel.
[12] Premium taxes on insurance are a significant source of revenue for states' general funds. In 2008, states collected approximately $15.7 billion in premium taxes. "2008 State Government Tax Collections" U.S. Census website http://www.census.gov/govs/statetax/historical_data_2008.html.
[13] Surplus lines insurance is insurance sold by insurers who are not licensed to sell insurance in particular state. See CRS Report RS22506, Surplus Lines Insurance: Background and Current Legislation, by Baird Webel, for more information on this insurance.
[14] H.R. 1180, Sec. 109 (a).

[15] A chart of various state regulations can be found at the website of the Insurance Information Institute, a property/casualty insurer organization. http://www.iii.org/media/hottopics/insurance/ratereg.

[16] Surplus lines insurance is insurance sold by insurers who are not licensed to sell insurance in particular state. See CRS Report RS22506, Surplus Lines Insurance: Background and Current Legislation, by Baird Webel, for more information on this insurance.

[17] A chart of various state regulations can be found at the website of the Insurance Information Institute, a property/casualty insurer organization, http://www.iii.org/media/hottopics/insurance/ratereg/?table_sort_575580=3.

[18] See, for example, "Chartering Bill Introduced; Industry Divided on Federal Proposal," Business Insurance, January 7, 2002, p. 1 and "Schumer working on Federal Regulation and Terrorism Backstop Bills in the Senate," BestWire, March 13, 2002.

[19] Draft Language can be found under "Testimony" at http://www.aba.com/ABIA/ABIA_Reg_Mod_Page.htm.

In: Insurance Regulation: Background and Issues ISBN: 978-1-62948-141-8
Editor: Nelson R. Phillips

Chapter 4

The Liability Risk Retention Act: Background, Issues, and Current Legislation*

Baird Webel

Summary

Risk retention groups (RRGs) and risk purchasing groups (RPGs) are alternative insurance entities authorized by Congress to expand insurance supply through a simplification of insurance regulation. The McCarran-Ferguson Act of 1945 generally leaves the regulation and taxation of the business of insurance to the individual states. In 1981 and 1986, however, Congress crafted a narrow exception to the usual state insurance regulations for these groups, generally exempting them from multiple state oversight. Membership in risk retention and purchasing groups is limited to commercial enterprises and governmental bodies, and the risks insured by these groups are limited to liability risks.

Over the past two decades, interest—both in Congress and in the market—in RRGs and RPGs has varied largely with the vagaries of the regular insurance market. From 2001 to 2004, the insurance market was in one of its periodic "hard" markets, and regular insurance became increasingly expensive and sometimes unavailable. Since 2001, the

* This is an edited, reformatted and augmented version of a Congressional Research Service publication, CRS Report for Congress RL32176, from www.crs.gov, prepared for Members and Committees of Congress, dated June 24, 2011.

numbers of risk retention groups rose dramatically and calls have been heard to expand the scope of insurance that they are allowed to offer. At the same time, some problems occurred in individual risk retention groups, and cautionary voices have also been raised. Although the liability insurance market has softened somewhat in the past few years, with policies becoming more available and relatively less expensive, risk retention groups have continued to form in significant numbers.

The fundamental question surrounding expansion of the Liability Risk Retention Act (LRRA) can be posed as an issue of availability vs. reliability. Those who would support expansion often emphasize a failure of the current insurance market and the current regulatory system to make a sufficient supply of insurance available so that consumers who need insurance can find it at a reasonable price. The question they pose is essentially: "What happens to a community when a business, a school, or a doctor can not afford or find liability insurance?" Those who would oppose expansion often emphasize the dangers in allowing insurance to be sold that is not subject to same regulatory standards as "normal" insurance. The question this group poses is essentially: "What happens to a community if the insurer from which this business, school, or doctor purchases insurance ends up insolvent or if the policy does not cover what needs to be covered?" In the 112th Congress, H.R. 2126, the Risk Retention Modernization Act of 2011, would extend the LRRA to commercial property insurance, authorize the Federal Insurance Office to determine the states' compliance with the act and impose corporate governance standards on RRGs and RPGs. Representative John Campbell introduced the bill on June 3, 2011. A similar bill was introduced in the 111th Congress by Representative Dennis Moore, with Representative Campbell as a cosponsor. This report outlines the current regulatory structures affecting risk retention and risk purchasing groups as well as the legislative and market history of these groups. It also discusses the debate regarding possible expansion of these groups into areas beyond commercial liability insurance.

INTRODUCTION

The insurance industry, particularly property/casualty insurance,[1] is known for alternating periods of "hard" and "soft" markets. Turns in this cycle are typically traced to unexpected changes in the investment climate, unexpected changes in insurance payouts, or both. During a typical hard market, the supply of insurance goes down, insurance prices go up, and underwriting standards become more stringent. This often leads to consumers encountering difficulty in finding and affording insurance. During a soft market, prices are typically flat, and insurers are more willing to underwrite greater risks, so consumers typically do not face such problems in obtaining insurance. Legislative attention tends to focus on insurance matters during hard markets as constituents relate complaints about finding or affording insurance to their legislators. Because regulation of the insurance market was left to the states in the McCarran-Ferguson Act of 1945,[2] however, the legislature in question is most often a state legislature. Among the solutions offered at the state level has been the creation of, or allowance for, "alternative" market entities to increase the amount of insurance available to consumers. The alternative market is made up of entities or arrangements that spread and finance risk like an insurance company, but that operate outside the normal regulations governing the world of "regular" insurance companies.[3]

In 1981, Congress authorized the creation of alternative market entities known as risk retention groups and risk purchasing groups (RRGs and RPGs). Their purpose was to expand insurance supply by simplifying state insurance regulation. In the 1981 act, subsequently amended in 1986 and known now as the Liability Risk Retention Act[4] (LRRA), Congress crafted a narrow exception to the usual state insurance regulations for these groups in largely exempting the groups from multiple state regulation. Over the past few years, interest in risk retention and purchasing groups has increased as access to affordable insurance has become a challenge for some businesses. Some have suggested that Congress needs to expand the narrow exception that was made in the 1980s in order to expand the supply of insurance in areas outside of the liability coverage allowed under the current law. Legislation was introduced in both the 110th and 111th Congresses to expand the LRRA to commercial property insurance, but no action was take on these bills. Such legislation (H.R. 2126) was introduced again in the 112th Congress by Representative John Campbell.

RECENT LEGISLATION

112th Congress

Risk Retention Modernization Act of 2011 (H.R. 2126)

H.R. 2126 was introduced by Representatives John Campbell, along with Representative Peter Welch, on June 3, 2011. It has been referred to the House Committee on Financial Services.

This bill would expand the federal preemption of state insurance laws, allowing risk retention groups to cover commercial property risks and risk purchasing groups to purchase coverage for commercial property risks. The bill would also change the enforcement mechanism for federal preemptions in the LRRA, and add additional federal corporate governance, disclosure, and fiduciary duty requirements for risk retention groups under the act.

Under existing law, the federal preemptions in the LRRA are enforced through court action. If a risk retention group believes a state is attempting to regulate in a manner counter to the LRRA, it can bring suit in a federal court. H.R. 2126 would create a process under which the director of the Federal Insurance Office could issue determinations as to whether a state's regulation of an RRG or RPG is preempted by the act. In addition, the director is to study and issue reports to Congress on the states' regulation of RRGs and RPGs and the compliance with the LRRA.

The corporate governance standards to be issued by the director of the Federal Insurance Office by the bill would include requirements that a majority of directors on an RRG's board be independent, any audit committee be made up of independent directors, written governance standards be in place, and contracts with service providers be limited to less than five years and be approved by the state insurance commissioner. Additional specific amendments to the LRRA would expand the consumer disclosure required in the act and impose a fiduciary duty on the board of directors of a risk retention group.

111th Congress

Risk Retention Modernization Act of 2010 (H.R. 4802)

H.R. 4802 was introduced by Representative Dennis Moore (along with Representatives John Campbell and Suzanne Kosmas) on March 10, 2010. It was referred to the House Committee on Financial Services but was not acted upon further. This bill was essentially similar to H.R. 2126 as introduced in the 112th Congress (detailed above). Differences include the replacement of the "Secretary of the Treasury" in H.R. 4802 with the "Director of the Federal Insurance Office"[5] as the primary federal official tasked with overseeing state compliance with federal law and the deletion of a section in H.R. 4802 calling for an study by the Comptroller General of the United States.

The sponsors of H.R. 4802, through a separate July 22, 2010, letter to the Comptroller General, requested that the Government Accountability Office

(GAO) conduct a study similar to the one required in H.R. 4802. According to Representative Moore's office, GAO indicated that such a study would be conducted, but it is unclear when the results may be issued.

110th Congress

Increasing Insurance Coverage Options for Consumers Act of 2008 (H.R. 5792)

H.R. 5792 was introduced by Representative Dennis Moore (along with Representatives Deborah Price, John Campbell, and Ron Klein) on April 15, 2008. It was addressed in an April 16 hearing "Examining Proposals on Insurance Regulatory Reform" held by the House Financial Services Subcommittee on Capital Markets, Insurance, and Government Sponsored Enterprises. The bill was marked up by this subcommittee on July 9, 2008, and forwarded to the full committee, but it was not acted on further in the 110th Congress.

H.R. 5792 would have expanded the LRRA exemptions to commercial property insurance. In addition, the bill would have implemented a number of corporate governance standards for RRGs, including requiring a majority of independent directors on an RRG's board, requiring an audit committee made up of independent directors, requiring a written charter, and limiting longer-term contracts with service providers. The bill would also have required all RRGs offering property coverage to be U.S.-licensed insurance companies.[6]

RISK RETENTION AND PURCHASING GROUP STRUCTURE AND REGULATION

Risk retention groups are required by current federal law[7] to be state-chartered insurance companies; they are allowed to insure commercial liability risks, such as the risk that a physician will be found liable for medical malpractice, but not other property/casualty risks, such as the risk that a physician's office might burn down. These insurance companies also must be owned by the members of the group. All policies issued by a risk retention group must bear a federally mandated warning that the policy is not regulated or guaranteed in the same way as other insurance. Group members are required to be businesses, including individual professionals such as physicians and attorneys, or government entities, such as public universities, school districts, and town or city administrations, who are engaged in a similar business or face similar risks. The exact corporate structure of a risk retention group can vary. Many are licensed as "captive" insurers,[8] which may have lower capital requirements, but some are licensed as "regular" mutual insurers. Risk purchasing groups are likewise groups of entities in a similar business or facing similar risks. Instead of creating their own insurance company, these groups join together to purchase commercial insurance from established insurance companies.

If risk retention groups must be licensed as an insurer under the existing laws of an individual state, two questions arise: What advantages do they possess? Why go to the trouble and expense of creating such a group? The answers are in the different regulatory treatment of these groups as they operate outside of the state where they are chartered (or "domiciled"). Under normal circumstances, an insurer who wishes to operate outside of its domiciliary state must receive a license and submit to regulation from every state in which it wishes to do business. This means complying with up to 51 different sets of state or district laws and regulations in order to do business across the country. The impact of this multiplicity of regulation is particularly high in insurance, as compared with other businesses, because both the prices and the content of insurance policies are highly regulated in most states. This perceived burden of multiple state regulatory systems is also the primary argument cited currently by some in the insurance industry for creating a federal charter to replace or supplement the current state system.[9]

Risk retention groups are exempted by federal law from the requirement to be licensed in all states in which they operate as well as from other state laws regulating the business of insurance. They must register and file documentation with a state's insurance regulator, but after this filing, they are essentially free to do business in that state. This exemption from state law extends to most laws on the business of insurance, but laws such as those on fraudulent trade practices, nondiscrimination, and unfair claim settlement practices still apply. Risk retention groups must also pay state premium taxes as regular insurers do. In addition, a non-domiciliary state's insurance regulator is empowered to monitor the financial solvency of a group, including requiring that a group submit to a financial condition examination if the chartering state regulator refuses to do such an exam, and seeking an injunction to force it to cease doing business if the group is in hazardous financial condition. This regulatory oversight is less than that accorded regular insurance companies, however, and some observers fear that this might lead to an increased danger of such groups becoming insolvent. In the case of a risk retention group insolvency, the policyholders have no recourse to a state guaranty fund because membership in these funds is specifically prohibited by the federal statute.

Risk purchasing groups are given a similar, but more limited, exemption from state law. Many states have laws, known as "fictitious grouping laws," that specifically prohibit or limit groups from purchasing insurance for the members of the group, particularly if the group exists solely for the purchase of insurance. State insurance regulators use these laws to protect consumers and ensure solvency. Risk purchasing groups are exempted from these laws and from countersignature laws, which are laws requiring a local broker's or agent's signature on an insurance contract. The insurance that such groups purchase on behalf of their members must meet the laws and regulations of the state that is designated as the domicile of that group.

LEGISLATIVE HISTORY

The 1981 Product Liability Risk Retention Act

The first "Product Liability Risk Retention Act" was introduced in 1979, and an amended version became P.L. 97-45 in 1981. Its origin can be traced to an interagency task force created by the White House in 1975[10] to examine difficulties in the availability of product liability insurance. Among the proposals discussed by the task force's report was the possible creation of alternatives to the traditional insurance market. The 1981 act was relatively narrow, limiting risk retention groups and risk purchasing groups to insurance covering product liability[11] as well as completed operations liability.[12] The 1981 act also limited members of these groups to "product manufacturers, wholesalers, distributors and retailers."[13] Risk retention groups had to be chartered, and thus regulated, as an insurer in one of the United States or U.S. jurisdictions, or in Bermuda or the Cayman Islands.[14] The act specifically exempted risk retention groups from most regulation by any state in which they operate, aside from the chartering state. This federal exemption, however, did not cover laws that were not specific to the business of insurance, such as fraud or deceptive practice laws. The act also preempted any state laws preventing risk purchasing groups from purchasing the same narrow range of insurance as that allowed to be offered by risk retention groups.

By the time the act became law in September 1981, the liability market difficulties that prompted so much attention had largely passed. With regular commercial insurance available and relatively inexpensive, there was little incentive for companies to undertake the expense of forming risk retention or purchasing groups, and only three of the former and four of the latter were formed in the first four years of the act's operation.

Despite the lack of market action, congressional interest in the issue continued. In 1983, a Clarification of the Risk Retention Act (S. 1046, eventually P.L. 98-193) was passed by voice votes of both the House and the Senate. This act was a response to a model state law promulgated by the National Association of Insurance Commissioners (NAIC).[15] This model law referenced the various state tort laws in its definition of "product liability" rather than following the definition passed by Congress in the 1981 act. The state tort laws tended to have a more narrow definition than that desired by Congress. P.L. 98-193 specified clearly that the definitions in the federal statute would be the controlling definitions for purposes of the Risk Retention Act.[16]

The 1986 Liability Risk Retention Act

In the mid-1980s, the insurance market began to harden again and Congress again heard of many problems faced by businesses and individuals in finding and affording insurance. One of the congressional responses was to reconsider the 1981 act. Numerous bills were introduced to expand the provisions so that more consumers might avail themselves of the additional insurance supply mechanism that Congress had created.

Congress ultimately passed S. 2129 (eventually P.L. 99-563), which renamed the 1981 act the "Liability Risk Retention Act" and brought the law to its present form. P.L. 99-563 expanded the scope of the insurance to include most types of commercial liability insurance and expanded the organizations that could form such groups to include any business as well as state or local governments or governmental entities as long as all the members of a single group were engaged in similar business activities or were exposed to similar risks. This expansion, however, did not retroactively include the small number of foreign-based risk retention groups. These groups, formed under the temporary authority described above, were allowed to continue in the area of product liability insurance but were not permitted to expand into other kinds of commercial liability insurance. P.L. 99-563 also included changes designed to allow some increased oversight of risk retention and purchasing groups, including the requirement to file documentation in non-chartering states, and the right of non-chartering commissioners to conduct examinations if the chartering state fails to do so and to seek injunctions against groups in a hazardous financial situation. In general, however, the intent of Congress remained to allow these groups to operate throughout the country while being regulated largely, if not solely, by a single state regulator, rather than facing 51 jurisdictions with different laws and regulatory styles.

RRGs and RPGs Since 1986

Growth in the Risk Retention Market[17]

Market reaction to the expansion of the law was relatively swift. By 1988, 52 risk retention groups had been created with more than 24,000 insured and a total premium amount of $250 million. (See the *Appendix* for a table containing complete risk retention group statistics) The number climbed to 79 in 1991 and then plateaued for the next 10 years, actually declining to 72 in 2001. The number of insureds and the total premium amount, however, continued to increase, reaching over 172,000 insureds and $944 million in premiums in 2001. Within the aggregate statistics, there was significant churning, as individual groups are formed and retired based on the business decisions made by those seeking insurance. In the period from 1987 to 2001, a total of 142 risk retention groups were formed and 73 retired. Reasons for a group retirement vary greatly. Some became insolvent, some changed status to become a regular insurer or were absorbed by a regular insurer, and some simply ceased operation when insurance on the regular market became more affordable.[18]

The relative calm in the marketplace that prevailed through the 1990s ended quickly with the hardening of the insurance market in 2001. This hard market has been ascribed to the downturn in both interest rates and the stock market as well as to unexpected losses, particularly the approximately $35 billion in insured losses due to the terrorist attacks on September 11, 2001. Making many of the price increases even more dramatic after 2001 was the prolonged soft market of the 1990s, which led to underpricing by insurers and some complacency on the part of the insured policyholders.

Interest in risk retention groups increased along with the prices of insurance and reinsurance. The number of RRGs and premiums increased fairly steadily from 72 groups and $994 million in premium in 2001 to 245 groups and $2.6 billion in premiums in 2006. The number of RRG insureds, however, did not follow the same pattern. The insureds numbered 172,713 in 2001, declining to 139,837 in 2002, before growing to nearly 218,000 in 2006. (This decline in insureds was due particularly to insolvencies in RRGs discussed below.)

Risk retention group growth during the hard market of the early 2000s occurred particularly in the health care arena. In the 2004 survey, for example, 28 of the 41 new groups were insuring some form of health care liability. In the 2007 study, the comparable number was 34 of 52 new RRGs. Within health care, nursing homes showed the largest growth, going from zero nursing home RRGs in 2002 to 20 at the end of 2005.[19] The growth in health care RRGs seemed largely due to widely reported difficulties that health care providers were encountering in obtaining medical malpractice insurance. In one interesting case, a Pennsylvania Department of Public Welfare grant reportedly provided the initial $5 million in capital for a Vermont-domiciled risk retention group with the purpose of insuring nursing homes solely in Pennsylvania.[20] Apparently, this occurred because the chartering laws on the creation of smaller or captive insurers in Vermont were preferred to those in Pennsylvania.

The liability insurance market generally has softened since 2005 or so.[21] For 2010, risk retention group premiums are estimated to have been approximately $2.7 billion, with 262 groups in operation and more than 272,000 insureds.[22]

Individual Difficulties Have Come Along with Growth

The growth of risk retention groups has not been without some problems. As was noted above, the number of insured declined from 2001 to 2004. This was largely due to the liquidation of three Tennessee-domiciled groups[23] that insured physicians, lawyers, and other professionals for professional liability. The liquidation was forced by the insolvency of a regular Virginia-based insurer who had provided reinsurance for these risk retention groups. Individual policyholders of regular insurance are normally eligible for protection in the case of insurer insolvency under the various states' guaranty funds; this, however, would typically apply only to those directly insured by the Virginia company, not to policyholders of companies that are reinsured by this company. These policyholders are considered creditors of the company, not insureds, and thus have a lower priority claim on the assets of the failed company. Further complicating the legal situation is the statutory prohibition on risk retention group participation in state guaranty funds. Class action lawsuits[24] were filed by insureds seeking guaranty fund protection for the insured along with damages for other malfeasance.[25]

Another risk retention group failure that has attracted considerable attention is the insolvency of the National Warranty Insurance Risk Retention Group (hereafter "National Warranty"). Although physically headquartered in Lincoln, Nebraska, National Warranty was incorporated in the Cayman Islands. It was one of a handful of RRGs that were incorporated outside of the United States before 1985 and was thus grandfathered out of regulation by any of the individual states. Prior to its being declared insolvent in August 2003, it acted as an insurer of the obligations taken on by its members, mainly marketing companies and auto dealerships, who sold vehicle service contracts. Although the actual group was made up of only approximately 580 members, the potential effect of the insolvency is more widespread, as these members sold contracts to or through more than 5,000 auto dealerships in 49 states.[26]

The text of the LRRA requires insureds to be members and part owners of a risk retention group; however, this line was apparently somewhat blurred in the National Warranty case. National Warranty acted both as an administrator, adjusting claims on behalf of its members, and as the insurer of these members.[27] This dual role apparently gave the impression that the final consumers were purchasing service contracts directly from National Warranty rather than from the individual group members. The National Warranty liquidation process is still ongoing.[28]

Policy Issues and Considerations

For several years, interest groups have made a concerted effort, including the formation of a Council for Expanding the Risk Retention Act, to advocate expanding the provisions of the Risk Retention Act to include commercial property and casualty insurance, except for workers' compensation insurance. In 2002, the National Conference of Insurance Legislators (NCOIL) approved a resolution supporting such an expansion, and a major consumer group, the Consumer Federation of America, has written in support of the idea as well.[29] Some insurance regulators, for example, then-District of Columbia Commissioner Lawrence Mirel and then-Vermont Director of Captive

Insurance Leonard Crouse, also previously expressed their support for expansion of the Risk Retention Act.[30]

Doubts about such an expansion, however, have also been raised. In National Association of Insurance Commissioners (NAIC) meetings, a prominent doubter was former Nebraska's insurance director, Tim Wagner, who was at the forefront of dealing with the National Warranty insolvency. At the September 2003 meeting, the NAIC was encouraged to adopt a draft resolution that would put the group on record as opposing the expansion of risk retention groups.[31] Among the reasons cited in the resolution was the danger to consumers from a limitation on states' regulatory authority, the example of the National Warranty failure, and the absence of an availability problem in property insurance that has not been addressed by state-based solutions. No resolution has been adopted, but a "Risk Retention Working Group" to examine issues surrounding risk retention groups was created. Among other actions, this group has proposed corporate governance standards for RRGs.[32] The U.S. Government Accountability Office also discussed problems in risk retention groups in a 2005 report entitled *Risk Retention Groups: Common Regulatory Standards and Greater Member Protections Are Needed.*[33]

The fundamental questions surrounding LRRA expansion are essentially the same as those addressed by Congress when the first act was passed in 1981, and when it was expanded in 1986. Stripping away jargon, this question can be phrased as an issue of availability vs. reliability. Arguments in support of expansion often focus on a failure of the current insurance market, and the current regulatory system, to make a sufficient supply of insurance available so that consumers who need insurance can find it at a reasonable price. The question posed is essentially: "What happens to a community when a business, a school, or a doctor cannot find or afford insurance?" Arguments opposing expansion often focus on the dangers in allowing insurance to be sold that is not subject to same regulatory standards as "normal" insurance. The question posed is essentially: "What happens to a community if the insurer from which this business, school, or doctor purchases insurance ends up bankrupt or if the policy does not cover what needs to be covered?" The underlying basis for this question with regard to risk retention groups seems to be the assumption that the single domiciliary state regulator will do an insufficient job in protecting the consumers who live in other states. Recent legislation in Congress has addressed some concerns raised in the past about the "reliability" of risk retention groups through the provisions addressing corporate governance structures and disclosure.

Secondary arguments are also made. Because the insured are the owners of a risk retention group, it could be argued that they can see to it themselves that the insurance provided is reliable. It is also argued that the rates of failure of regular insurers and risk retention groups are nearly the same, and that the failure of National Warranty was a unique situation since it was an offshore group that was unaccountable to any state regulator. Doubters may counter by questioning what sort of impact risk retention groups might have when, even with their recent growth, they still occupy a fraction of a percent of the property/casualty market.

In addition, even if the failure rates are similar, the impact of a state-regulated insurer failure is likely to be mitigated by its participation in state guaranty funds, which are specifically unavailable to insurers operating under the Liability Risk Retention Act.

Assessing the arguments on either side is a challenge for Congress. The broad question of availability vs. reliability can be framed by some as a basic philosophical question about the degree of regulation needed by insurance markets and may not have an absolute empirical answer. Some see insurance philosophically as a public good, akin to a basic utility, and one that must be highly regulated in price and content to protect consumers. Others do not share this philosophy and feel insurance should be lightly regulated, with the market determining prices and content. In general, the states, who have faced such basic insurance regulatory questions for many years, have attempted to suit the amount of regulation to the perceived sophistication of the consumer. Thus, the market for commercial insurance is usually left relatively less regulated on the theory that the businesses purchasing in the commercial market have the knowledge and experience to discern the intricacies of insurance policies and companies, or at least hire professionals to make these "reliability" judgments for them. Individual consumers are presumed to be less well placed to make these judgments; thus, the market for such insurance, particularly homeowners and auto, tends to be more regulated. Internationally, the insurance markets in general have tended to be less regulated, particularly with regard to the direct price and content controls found in some of the United States.[34]

The differential regulatory approach based on the sophistication of the consumer can be seen, for example, in the operation of state guaranty funds. These funds are intended to step in and pay claims arising from insolvent insurers, but they typically have a relatively low cap on the amount that can be paid to each policyholder. Keeping this amount low implies that consumers with relatively low claims, presumably most individuals, will be nearly fully protected against loss, while consumers with relatively high claims, presumably larger businesses, will be only partially protected. This cap on guaranty fund claims also affects the direct arguments surrounding risk retention groups. Because most risk retention group members, as businesses, face potentially large claims, the value of guaranty fund protection will be less to them than to individuals with presumably lower claims.

In assessing some of the more factual arguments, it is true that risk retention and purchasing groups occupy a small part of the insurance market. The approximately $422 billion[35] total premium written in the property/casualty market in 2009 was many times the approximately $2.5 billion in risk retention group premium. Economic theory suggests, however, that it is not necessary for a competitor to have a large market share in order to have an impact on prices or availability. Anecdotal cases, particularly ones such as the Pennsylvania nursing home risk retention group mentioned above, also suggest that the act is expanding the availability of insurance, especially in local situations with severe supply difficulties. The Department of Commerce came to the conclusion in 1989 that the 1986 act had been successful in addressing supply problems,[36] and the GAO made similar findings in the previously mentioned 2005 report.[37]

An assessment of risk retention and purchasing groups also may offer insight into wider questions involving the federal role in insurance regulation. Particularly since the passage of 1999's Gramm-Leach-Bliley Act,[38] some have advocated for an increased federal role in insurance regulation, up to complete federalization of regulation for all interstate insurers.

Others have suggested some lesser federal role to address specific problems they see caused by the multiplicity of state regulators, such as slow approval times for products and overly burdensome rate or form regulation. The recent Dodd-Frank Wall Street Reform and Consumer Protection Act[39] includes some insurance provisions, but the debate over the federal role in insurance is expected to continue in the future.[40] The two Risk Retention Acts are an example of one way previous Congresses have tried to solve supply problems arising from, or exacerbated by, the insurance regulatory system.

The answer provided by these acts was essentially a system of enforced mutual state recognition without broad federal regulation of insurance. As such an example, these acts might provide some insight into how Congress considers addressing problems in the insurance regulatory system today.

APPENDIX. RISK RETENTION GROUPS STATISTICS

Table A-1. Risk Retention Groups, 1988-2010

Year	Number of RRGs	Premium Total (millions of $)	Number of Insureds
1988	52	$250.2	24,464
1989	66	$393.4	31,219
1990	76	$452.8	47,857
1991	79	$493.6	46,789
1992	80	$493.7	53,088
1993	85	$527.2	48,849
1994	84	$585.3	63,978
1995	78	$575.5	64,211
1996	73	$707.6	119,269
1997	74	$751.9	150,802
1998	73	$764.4	158,851
1999	73	$769.5	163,235
2000	69	$802.8	165,120
2001	72	$944.0	172,713
2002	90	$1,265.1	139,837
2003	148	$1,737.7	145,582
2004	195	$2,197.7	154,845
2005	219	$2,449.1	197,420
2006	245	$2,638.6	217,924
2007	265	$2,559.1	226,879
2008	272	$2,575.0	238,112
2009	270	$2,638.4	257,720
2010 (projected)	261	$2,683.2	272,223

Source: Annual Surveys by the Risk Retention Reporter.

End Notes

[1] The insurance industry is typically broken down into life/health and property/casualty insurance. Life/health is relatively straightforward, following its name, and also includes annuity products. Property/casualty is a more diverse group, including auto, homeowners, professional liability, and many others. Property/casualty essentially refers to everything that is not life or health insurance.

[2] 15 U.S.C. §§ 1011 et seq, P.L. 79-15, 59 Stat. 33.

[3] See Insurance Information Institute, "Captives and Other Risk-Financing Options," at http://www.iii.org/media/ hottopics/insurance/test3.

[4] 15 U.S.C. §§ 3901-3906, created by P.L. 97-45 and P.L. 99-563.

[5] The Federal Insurance Office was not in existence when H.R. 4802 was introduced.

[6] The 1981 Risk Retention Act allowed offshore risk retention groups. The 1986 amendments required RRGs be domiciled in the United States, but grandfathered the small number of then-existing offshore RRGs.

[7] 15 U.S.C. 3901 et seq.

[8] Captive insurers are "Insurers that are created and wholly owned by one or more non-insurers, to provide owners with coverage. A form of self-insurance." From the Insurance Information Institute's online glossary available http://www2.iii.org/glossary/c/. See also http://www.captive.com. Captives are typically licensed as insurers either in an individual state or offshore, often in Bermuda or the Cayman Islands.

[9] For more information on the federal chartering issue, see CRS Report RL34286, Insurance Regulation: Federal Charter Legislation, by Baird Webel.

[10] Interagency Task Force on Product Liability. Its final report was published by the Department of Commerce in 1977 (NTIS PB-273-320).

[11] "Products liability refers to the liability of a manufacturer or seller for injury caused by his product to the person or property of a buyer or third party." See CRS Report R40148, Products Liability: A Legal Overview, by Vivian S. Chu for additional discussion.

[12] Completed operations liability insurance generally covers claims arising after the completion of a project (for example, if a contractor finished a house, but a defect was found some time later).

[13] U.S. Congress, Senate Committee on Commerce, Science, and Transportation, Product Liability Risk Retention Act of 1981, report to accompany S. 1096, 97th Cong., 1st sess., S.Rept. 97-102 (Washington, GPO, 1981), p. 1; and U.S. Congress, House Committee on Energy and Commerce, Product Liability Risk Retention Act of 1981, report to accompany H.R. 2120, 97th Cong., 1st sess., H.Rept. 97-190 (Washington, GPO, 1981), p. 7.

[14] The authority to form risk retention groups outside of the United States was limited in time, expiring on January 1, 1985.

[15] The NAIC is the national trade association of state insurance regulators, which, among other activities, publishes model laws to encourage harmonization of state insurance regulation.

[16] For more discussion, see U.S. Congress, Senate Committee on Commerce, Science, and Technology, Clarification of the Risk Retention Act, report to accompany S. 1046, 98th Cong., 1st sess., S.Rept. 98-172 (Washington, GPO, 1983).

[17] Except where noted, statistics in the section taken from successive annual surveys done by the Risk Retention Reporter (Pasadena, CA; http://rrr.com/).

[18] See "Soft Market Fueled Risk Retention Group Retirements During 1990s," Risk Retention Reporter, February 2002.

[19] "Premium Generated By Healthcare RRGs More Than Triples Since 2001," Risk Retention Reporter, December 2002.

[20] Andrew Sargeant, USA Risk Group of Vermont, as quoted in "Sources of Capital for Risk Retention Groups," Risk Retention Reporter, June, 2003.

[21] Some other insurance markets, particularly the property insurance market in states threatened by hurricanes, have significantly hardened in the past few years. This has prompted Congress to explore other avenues to expand insurance supply, such as The Homeowners' Defense Act of 2009 (S. 505/H.R. 2555 in the 111th Congress). See CRS Report R40680, Financing Catastrophic Risk: Summary of the Homeowners' Defense Act of 2009 (S. 505 and H.R. 2555), by Rawle O. King.

[22] "Premium and Number of RRGs by Business Area," The Risk Retention Reporter, October 2010.

[23] These groups were the American National Lawyers Insurance Reciprocal, Doctors Insurance Reciprocal Risk Retention Group, and The Reciprocal Alliance.

[24] Fullen v. General Reinsurance Corp., et al. (VLW 003-12-03), Herrick v. General Reinsurance Corp., et al. (VLW 003-12-01), and Crenshaw Community Hospital v. General Reinsurance Corp., et al. (VLW 003-12-02). See "Class-Action Suits Filed Against Reciprocal Companies," Virginia Lawyers Weekly, April 3, 2003, available at http://www.valawyers weekly.com/anlir14.cfm. These three suits were subsequently consolidated in the United States District Court for the Middle District of Tennessee (Memphis) as In re Reciprocal of America (ROA) Sales Practices Litigation (MDL No. 1551).

[25] For a more complete reporting, see "Policyholders of Reinsurance Group Reciprocal to Get Partial Payment," Richmond Times-Dispatch, October 20, 2003, and "Move to Liquidate ROA Will Impact RRG Insureds and Others," Risk Retention Reporter, May 2003, as well as the previously cited article in Virginia Lawyers Weekly.

[26] Figures from John Taylor, "Irate Consumers File Class-Action Suit against Lincoln, Neb., Firm," Omaha World-Herald, September 23, 2003.

[27] Caroline McDonald, "Lessons from National Warranty," National Underwriter, Property & Casualty/Risk & Benefits Management Edition, October 24, 2003.

[28] See the company website at http://www.nwig.com.

[29] See Consumer Federation of America, Creating Insurance Alternatives to Bring Down Rates, at http://www.consumerfed.org/pdfs/risk_retention_act-expansion.PDF.

[30] Lawrence Mirel, letter To Whom It May Concern, September 16, 2002, and Leonard Crouse, letter To Whom It May Concern, May 15, 2002.

[31] Meg Fletcher, "NAIC May Seek to Block RRG Expansion," BI Daily News, September 18, 2003, at http://www.businessinsurance.com/cgi-bin/news.pl?newsId=2894.

[32] The NAIC Risk Retention Group Task Force's recent activities can be found on the NAIC website at http://www.naic.org/committees_e_risk_retention_group_tf.htm.

[33] U.S. Government Accountability Office, Risk Retention Groups: Common Regulatory Standards and Greater Member Protections Are Needed, GAO-05-536, August 2005, available at http://www.gao.gov/new.items/d05536.pdf.

[34] For a more in-depth discussion of insurance regulation, see CRS Report R40771, Insurance Regulation: Issues, Background, and Legislation in the 111th Congress, by Baird Webel.

[35] See the Insurance Information Institute website at http://www2.iii.org/financial/insurance/allsectors.

[36] See U.S. Department of Commerce, Liability Risk Retention Act of 1986: Operations Report 1989, NTIS PB 90- 123134.

[37] "RRGs have had a small but important effect in increasing the availability and affordability of commercial liability insurance for certain groups." U.S. Government Accountability Office, Risk Retention Groups: Common Regulatory Standards and Greater Member Protections Are Needed, GAO-05-536, August 2005, p. 5.

[38] P.L. 106-102, 113 Stat. 1338.

[39] P.L. 111-203; see also CRS Report R41372, The Dodd-Frank Wall Street Reform and Consumer Protection Act: Insurance Provisions, by Baird Webel.

[40] See, for example "Frank: Federal Charter Debate on Tap in 2011," BestWire, July 8, 2010.

In: Insurance Regulation: Background and Issues ISBN: 978-1-62948-141-8
Editor: Nelson R. Phillips

Chapter 5

THE DODD-FRANK WALL STREET REFORM AND CONSUMER PROTECTION ACT: INSURANCE PROVISIONS*

Baird Webel

SUMMARY

In the aftermath of the recent financial crisis, broad financial regulatory reform legislation was advanced by the Obama Administration and by various Members of Congress. Ultimately Congress passed, and the President signed, the Dodd-Frank Wall Street Reform and Consumer Protection Act (P.L. 111-203).

The Dodd-Frank Act largely responded to the financial crisis that peaked in September 2008, but other efforts at revising the state-based system of insurance regulation also pre-date this crisis. Members of Congress previously introduced both broad legislation to federalize insurance regulation along the lines of the regulation of the banking sector, as well as more narrowly tailored bills addressing specific perceived flaws in the state-based system.

The financial crisis, particularly the role of insurance giant American International Group (AIG) and the smaller bond insurers, changed the tenor of the existing debate around insurance regulation, with increased

---

* This is an edited, reformatted and augmented version of a Congressional Research Service publication, CRS Report for Congress R41372, prepared for Members and Committees of Congress, from www.crs.gov, dated August 17, 2010.

emphasis on the systemic importance of some insurance companies. Although it could be argued that insurer involvement in the financial crisis suggested a need for full-scale federal regulation of insurance, the Dodd-Frank Act did not implement such a federal regulatory system for insurance.

Title V of the Dodd-Frank Act addressed specifically insurance, with a subtitle creating a Federal Insurance Office (similar to language originally contained in H.R. 2609) and a subtitle streamlining the existing state regulation of surplus lines and reinsurance (similar to language originally contained in H.R. 2572/S. 1363). The Federal Insurance Office is to monitor all aspects of the insurance industry and coordinate and develop policy relating to international agreements. It also has limited authority to preempt state laws and regulations when these conflict with international agreements. The act harmonizes, and in some cases reduces, regulation and taxation of surplus lines insurance by vesting the "home state" of the insured with the sole authority to regulate and collect the taxes on a surplus lines transaction. For reinsurance transactions, the act vests the home state of the insurer purchasing the reinsurance with the authority over the transaction while vesting the home state of the reinsurer with the sole authority to regulate the solvency of the reinsurer.

In addition to Title V's specific insurance provisions, various other parts of the act may affect insurers and the insurance industry, including provisions addressing systemic risk, consumer protection, investor protection, and securities regulation.

This report explains how insurance markets were affected by the financial crisis and summarizes the provisions of the Dodd-Frank Act that pertain to insurance.

INSURANCE AND THE FINANCIAL CRISIS

Under the McCarran-Ferguson Act of 1945,[1] insurance regulation is generally left to the individual states. For several years prior to the recent financial crisis, some Members of Congress had introduced legislation to federalize insurance regulation along the lines of the regulation of the banking sector, although none of this legislation reached the committee markup stage.[2] Various other pieces of legislation have also been introduced to reform insurance regulation in more narrow ways.[3] The debate around federal involvement in insurance regulation had traditionally focused on the negative and positive aspects of the state-centered approach compared to increased federal government involvement.

The recent financial crisis, particularly the involvement of insurance giant American International Group (AIG) and the smaller bond insurers, changed the tenor of the debate around insurance regulation. The crisis grew largely from sectors of the financial industry that had previously been perceived as presenting little systemic risk. Many see the crisis as resulting from failures or gaps in the financial regulatory structure, particularly a lack of oversight for the system as a whole and a lack of coordinated oversight for the largest actors in the system.[4] This increased urgency in calls for overall regulatory changes, such as the implementation of increased systemic risk regulation and federal oversight of insurance, particularly of larger insurance firms. Generally good performance of insurers through the crisis, however, has also provided additional arguments for those seeking to retain the state-based insurance system.

Although insurers in general appear to have weathered the financial crisis reasonably well, the insurance industry saw two significant failures, one general and one specific. The first failure involved financial guarantee or "monoline" bond insurers. Before the crisis, there were only about a dozen bond insurers in total, with four large insurers[5] dominating the business. This type of insurance originated in the 1970s to cover municipal bonds, but the insurers expanded their businesses since the 1990s to include significant amounts of mortgage-backed securities. In late 2007 and early 2008, strains appeared due to exposure to mortgage-backed securities. Ultimately some smaller bond insurers failed and the larger insurers saw their previously triple-A credit ratings downgraded significantly. These downgrades rippled throughout the municipal bond markets, causing unexpected difficulties for both individual investors and municipalities who might have thought they were relatively insulated from problems stemming from rising mortgage defaults.

The second failure in the insurance industry was that of a specific company, AIG.[6] AIG had been a global giant of the industry, but it essentially failed in mid-September 2008. To avoid bankruptcy in September and October 2008, AIG was forced to seek more than $100 billion in assistance from, and give 79.9% of the equity in the company to, the Federal Reserve. Multiple restructurings of the assistance have followed, including up to $69.8 billion through the U.S. Treasury's Troubled Asset Relief Program (TARP). AIG is currently in the process of selling off parts of its business to pay back assistance that it has received from the government; how much value will be left in the 79.9% government stake in the company at the end of the process remains an open question.

The near collapse of the bond insurers and AIG could be construed as regulatory failures. One of the responsibilities of an insurance regulator is to ensure that insurers remain solvent and are able to pay future claims. Because the states are the primary insurance regulators, some may go further and argue that these cases specifically demonstrate the need for increased federal involvement in insurance. The case of AIG, however, is complicated. AIG was primarily made up of state-chartered insurance subsidiaries, but the state insurance regulators did not oversee the entire company. At the holding company level, AIG was a federally regulated thrift holding company and thus overseen by the Office of Thrift Supervision (OTS). The immediate losses that caused AIG's failure came from both derivatives operations overseen by OTS and from securities lending operations that originated with securities from state-chartered insurance companies. OTS claimed that it had sufficient regulatory authority and competence to oversee a complicated holding company such as AIG. Others, particularly the Federal Reserve, disputed this claim and argued that a single body is needed to oversee systemic risk and large financial holding companies.

THE DODD-FRANK WALL STREET REFORM AND CONSUMER PROTECTION ACT (P.L. 111-203)

The Dodd-Frank Act was passed in the House on June 30, 2010, by vote of 237-192, and in the Senate, on July 15, 2010, by a vote of 60-39. President Obama signed the legislation, now P.L. 111-203, on July 21, 2010.

Federal Insurance Office

Title V, Subtitle A of the Dodd-Frank Act creates a Federal Insurance Office (FIO) inside of the Department of the Treasury. A similar office was previously proposed in a 2008 Treasury "Blueprint for a Modernized Financial Regulatory Structure,"[7] in H.R. 5840 in the 110th Congress, and in H.R. 2609 in the 111th Congress.

FIO is to monitor all aspects of the insurance industry and coordinate and develop policy relating to international agreements. It has the authority to preempt state laws and regulations when these conflict with international agreements. This preemption authority is somewhat limited. It can only apply when the state measure (1) results in less favorable treatment of a non-U.S. insurer compared with a U.S. insurer, and (2) is inconsistent with a written international agreement regarding prudential measures. Such an agreement must achieve a level of consumer protection that is "substantially equivalent"[8] to the level afforded under state law. FIO preemption authority does not extend to state measures governing rates, premiums, underwriting, or sales practices, nor does it apply to state coverage requirements or state antitrust laws. FIO preemption decisions are also subject to *de novo* judicial review under the Administrative Procedures Act.[9] The monitoring function of FIO includes information gathering from both public and private sources. This is backed by subpoena power if the director issues a written finding that the information being sought is necessary and that the office has coordinated with other state or federal regulators that may have the information.

Consumer Financial Protection[10]

Title X of the Dodd-Frank Act creates a Bureau of Consumer Financial Protection within the Federal Reserve. This bureau enjoys significant budgetary independence, and the director is to be appointed by the President and confirmed by the Senate. Consumer protection issues relating to the business of insurance, however, do not fall under the oversight of the bureau, but would remain within the purview of the states. Consumer protection issues that relate to insurance products that are also considered securities continue to be addressed by the Securities and Exchange Commission (SEC).

Investor Protection and Securities Provisions[11]

Although insurance products are generally under state regulation, there are some products, particularly variable annuities, that are considered securities products under federal law and jointly overseen by the SEC. In 2008, the SEC adopted new rules, generally known as "Rule 151A," that would have expanded SEC oversight to include some fixed indexed annuities that previously had solely been overseen by the states as insurance products. This rule provoked controversy, with Representative Gregory Meeks and Senator Benjamin Nelson introducing the Fixed Indexed Annuities and Insurance Products Classification Act of 2009 (H.R. 2733/S. 1389) to overturn Rule 151A. H.R. 4173 included no provisions addressing Rule 151A as it moved through consideration in the House, and neither did S. 3217 in the Senate. Senator Tom Harkin proposed S.Amdt. 3920, which would have added the text of H.R. 2733/S. 1389 to S. 3217; but the amendment was not considered on the floor of the Senate.

The conference committee agreed to an amendment by Senator Harkin, contained in Section 989J of the act, that did not insert the previous language specifically nullifying Rule 151A, but is broadly aimed at returning indexed annuities solely to state oversight. The exemption from SEC oversight in Section 989J depends in part on either the states or the companies meeting certain consumer protection standards. Depending on future regulatory action by the SEC, this exemption language may require court action before the full impact of Section 989J is known.

In addition to the language on annuities, Section 913 of the act may affect some insurance producers who also sell security products. This section authorizes the SEC to establish a fiduciary duty for broker-dealers who give personalized investment advice. SEC-registered investment advisers are already subject to a fiduciary duty, which requires them to act in their customers' best interests. Broker-dealer recommendations, on the other hand, must be suitable for customers; the act directs the SEC to harmonize the standards applicable to broker-dealers and investment advisers. This provision is of interest to the insurance industry because agents who sell securities products, such as mutual funds or variable annuities, have been required to register as broker-dealers, but not generally as investment advisers. If the SEC issues rules creating a fiduciary duty, such agents will have to meet the best-interests standard that applies to advisers.

Systemic Risk Provisions[12]

The Dodd-Frank Act provides for systemic risk provisions that affect the insurance industry primarily through oversight of firms deemed systemically significant and through specific financial resolution authority. Financial companies, including insurers, judged to be systemically significant by the Financial Stability Oversight Council are to be subject to Federal Reserve oversight and higher prudential standards. The council includes a presidential appointee who is to be familiar with insurance issues, a state insurance commissioner, and the director of the Federal Insurance Office with the latter two being non-voting members.

Section 619 of the Dodd-Frank Act includes restrictions on proprietary trading by banking entities, a provision commonly known as the "Volcker Rule." Insurers that have banking subsidiaries or who are under a holding company structure with other banking subsidiaries would be subject to these restrictions, potentially affecting the investment strategies of these insurers. The language, however, includes an exemption for trading done "by a regulated insurance company directly engaged in the business of insurance for the general account of the company by any affiliate of such regulated insurance company, provided that such activities by any affiliate are solely for the general account of the regulated insurance company."[13] The transactions must also comply with applicable law, regulation, or guidance; and there must be no determination by the regulators that a relevant law, regulation, or guidance is insufficient to protect the safety and soundness of the banking entity or the financial stability of the United States.[14]

A financial company could be subject to the act's special resolution regime based on a finding that its failure would cause systemic risk. Any insurance subsidiaries of such a financial company, however, would not be subject to this regime. Instead, the resolution of insurance companies would continue to be conducted in accordance with the applicable state insurance resolution system.

With regard to funding for the resolution of systemically significant financial firms, there is no pre-funded resolution mechanism under the act. Instead, the Federal Deposit Insurance Corporation (FDIC) is to impose assessments on financial companies with more than $50 billion in assets, as well as other financial firms that are overseen by the Federal Reserve, to fund the resolution of a systemically significant firm in the event the assets of the failed firm are insufficient to do so. The FDIC is to impose such assessments on a risk-adjusted basis. When imposing such assessments on an insurance company, the FDIC is to take into account the insurers' contributions to the state insurance resolution regimes.

Surplus Lines and Reinsurance[15]

Title V, Subtitle B of the Dodd-Frank Act is entitled the Nonadmitted and Reinsurance Reform Act of 2010 and includes essentially the same language as H.R. 2571/S. 1361. Similarly titled bills were introduced in the 109th and 110th Congresses and passed the House, but were not considered by the Senate.

This language addresses a relatively narrow set of insurance regulatory issues pre-dating the financial crisis. In the area of nonadmitted (or "surplus lines") insurance, the act harmonizes, and in some cases reduces, regulation and taxation of this insurance by vesting the "home state" of the insured with the sole authority to regulate and collect the taxes on a surplus lines transaction. Those taxes that would be collected may be distributed according to a future interstate compact, but absent such a compact their distribution would be within the authority of the home state. It also preempts any state laws on surplus lines eligibility that conflict with the National Association of Insurance Commissioners (NAIC) model law and implements "streamlined" federal standards allowing a commercial purchaser to access surplus lines insurance. For reinsurance transactions, it vests the home state of the insurer purchasing the reinsurance with the authority over the transaction while vesting the home state of the reinsurer with the sole authority to regulate the solvency of the reinsurer.

End Notes

[1] 15 U.S.C. Sec. 1011 et seq.

[2] See CRS Report RL34286, Insurance Regulation: Federal Charter Legislation, by Baird Webel.

[3] See CRS Report R40771, Insurance Regulation: Issues, Background, and Legislation in the 111th Congress, by Baird Webel.

[4] See, for example, the remarks by SEC Chairman Mary L. Schapiro from the University of Rochester's Presidential Symposium on the Future of Financial Regulation, available at http://www.sec.gov/news/speech/2009/ spch101009mls.htm.

[5] Ambac, FGIC, FSA, and MBIA.

[6] See CRS Report R40438, Ongoing Government Assistance for American International Group (AIG), by Baird Webel.

[7] See U.S. Treasury, "Treasury Releases Blueprint for Stronger Regulatory Structure," press release, March 31, 2008, http://www.ustreas.gov/press/releases/hp896.htm.

[8] 31 U.S.C. §313(f)(2) as added by P.L. 111-203 §502; the law renumbers the current 31 U.S.C. sec. 313 as 31 U.S.C. Sec. 312.

[9] 5 U.S.C. §551 et seq.

[10] See CRS Report R41338, The Dodd-Frank Wall Street Reform and Consumer Protection Act: Title X, The Consumer Financial Protection Bureau, by David H. Carpenter.

[11] See CRS Report RS22974, Annuities and the Securities and Exchange Commission Rule 151A, by Baird Webel.

[12] See CRS Report R40877, Financial Regulatory Reform: Systemic Risk and the Federal Reserve, by Marc Labonte.

[13] P.L. 111-203 §619(d)(1)(F).

[14] This description is from CRS Report R41298, The "Volcker Rule": Proposals to Limit "Speculative" Proprietary Trading by Banks, by David H. Carpenter and M. Maureen Murphy; please see this report for additional information on the proposal.

[15] See CRS Report RS22506, Surplus Lines Insurance: Background and Current Legislation, by Baird Webel.

In: Insurance Regulation: Background and Issues ISBN: 978-1-62948-141-8
Editor: Nelson R. Phillips

Chapter 6

SURPLUS LINES INSURANCE: BACKGROUND AND CURRENT LEGISLATION*

Baird Webel

SUMMARY

In general, insurance is a highly regulated financial product. Every state requires licenses for insurance companies, and most states closely regulate both company conduct and the details of the particular insurance products sold in the state. This regulation is usually seen as important for consumer protection; however, it also creates barriers to entry in the insurance market and typically reduces to some degree the supply of insurance that is available to consumers. Rather than requiring consumers who may be unable to find insurance from a licensed insurer to simply go without insurance, states have allowed consumers to purchase insurance from non-licensed insurers, commonly called nonadmitted or surplus lines insurers. Although any sort of insurance could be sold by a surplus lines insurer, most such transactions tend to be for rarer and more exceptional property and casualty risks, such as art and antiques, hazardous materials, natural disasters, amusement parks, and environmental or pollution risks.

Although surplus lines insurance is sold by insurers who do not hold a regular state insurance license, it is not unregulated. The sale of this

* This is an edited, reformatted and augmented version of a Congressional Research Service publication, CRS Report for Congress RS22506, prepared for Members and Committees of Congress, from www.crs.gov, dated July 22, 2010.

insurance is regulated and taxed by the states largely through requirements placed on the brokers who usually facilitate the insurance transactions. The varying state requirements for surplus lines insurance have led to calls for greater harmonization between the states' laws and for federal intervention to promote uniformity. Such federal intervention is the central focus of the Nonadmitted and Reinsurance Reform Act of 2009 (H.R. 2571/S. 1363), which passed the House by voice vote on September 9, 2009. This act was also added as an amendment to the Wall Street Reform and Consumer Protection Act of 2009 (H.R. 4173) when it was considered on the House floor. H.R. 4173 passed the House on December 11, 2009. The Restoring America's Financial Stability Act of 2010 (S. 3217) included nearly identical language as well. This legislation was reported by the Senate Committee on Banking, Housing, and Urban Affairs on April 15, 2010, and subsequently brought to the Senate floor for consideration. On May 20, 2010, the Senate finished consideration, inserting the amended text of S. 3217 into H.R. 4173 and passing the amended H.R. 4173. The Nonadmitted and Reinsurance Reform Act language was included in the H.R. 4173 conference report, which was agreed to by the House on June 30, 2010, and by the Senate on July 15, 2010. President Obama signed the legislation, now P.L. 111-203, on July 21, 2010.

Provisions aimed at harmonizing state laws regarding surplus lines insurance were also included in the National Insurance Consumer Protection Act (H.R. 1880), whose central focus is the creation of a federal charter for the insurance industry when this bill was introduced on April 2, 2009.

Past Congresses have also taken up legislation on surplus lines insurance. Versions of the Nonadmitted and Reinsurance Reform Act were passed by the House in both the 109th and 110th Congresses, but the Senate did not act on surplus lines legislation in either case. Provisions on surplus lines insurance similar to those in H.R. 1880 were included in the National Insurance Act of 2007, but that bill was not acted on in the 110th Congress.

BACKGROUND ON INSURANCE REGULATION[1]

Insurance is regulated almost exclusively at a state level, unlike the other primary sectors of the financial services industry, banking and securities. Although the Supreme Court has ruled that Congress has the power to regulate insurance, the 1945 McCarran-Ferguson Act[2] devolved this power to the individual states, and this was specifically reaffirmed in the 1999 Gramm-LeachBliley Act.[3] It has long been recognized that some uniformity in insurance regulation is desirable as it allows greater efficiencies in the insurance market. This argument has grown stronger as insurers compete more with banks and securities firms, who do have uniform regulation, and as capital markets have become more globalized. Insurers rely increasingly on global capital markets both as a place to invest premiums that are not quickly paid out in claims and as a source of funding, particularly after a catastrophe that causes large losses.

Recognizing the need for relatively standardized regulation, the individual states have developed model rules and regulations through the National Association of Insurance Commissioners (NAIC) and the National Conference of Insurance Legislators (NCOIL). Harmonization efforts by the states, however, have been hampered by the lack of authority invested in either the NAIC or NCOIL. Although both are made up of public officials, the organizations themselves are voluntary, non-governmental associations and cannot require that any states enact their models. As a consequence, there is significant variation in how different states regulate insurance and there have been various calls for Congress to act through a federal charter or some other kind of federal intervention. The recent financial crisis added an additional argument for increased federal attention to the regulation of insurance, particularly with the failure of AIG, a company that happened to be the largest surplus lines insurer in the United States.

REGULATION OF SURPLUS LINES INSURANCE

Surplus lines insurance regulation differs from other insurance regulation both in substance and in the primary focus. In regulating regular insurance transactions, much of the state's focus is on the insurer itself. States have specific requirements for financial solvency, including how much capital an insurer must hold, and how the insurer can invest this capital. In cases of insolvency, states have established guaranty funds, funded by the rest of the insurers in the marketplace, to pay off the insolvent insurer's claims. The states also regulate both the substance of an insurance policy and the price of that policy, with many states requiring specific state approval before policy terms or prices can be changed. In surplus lines insurance, states have some oversight on the solvency of insurers, generally requiring that financial information be filed by surplus lines insurers to judge whether the insurers are sufficiently capitalized. There is, however, no participation in state guaranty funds by surplus lines insurers, nor state oversight of policy terms and prices charged.

Most surplus lines transactions revolve around an intermediary, typically an insurance broker, who may specialize in the unusual risks that require such coverage. Because they have relatively little oversight on surplus lines insurers themselves, the states generally focus their attention on these intermediaries in regulating surplus lines insurance. To operate as a surplus lines broker, most states require an additional license on top of the license required for insurance brokers in general. To retain this license, surplus lines brokers are required to take various steps with surplus lines transactions that are not required in regular insurance.

The first step in a surplus lines transaction is generally a state-required "diligent search" of the regular insurance marketplace to establish that there is no licensed insurer available to offer the required coverage. Typically, this requirement is satisfied by having some number, usually three to five, licensed insurers decline to offer coverage with the broker being responsible for an affidavit describing the search and certifying that no coverage is available in the licensed market. In some cases, states have established lists of coverages that are almost always placed in the surplus lines market and thus are exempt from the diligent search requirements.

Once the consumer's eligibility to use the surplus lines marketplace is established following whatever state rules are in place, the broker would then approach various surplus lines insurers seeking the desired coverage at a suitable price. At this point, while the consumer is outside of the regular insurance market, the states generally continue to establish standards to protect consumers against surplus lines insurers who might be unable to pay claims that are made. Some states establish a list of eligible surplus lines insurers, and state-licensed brokers are only allowed to transact with insurers on that list. Others take the opposite approach and issue a list of ineligible insurers that may not be used by state-licensed brokers. A third approach is to make the brokers responsible if a surplus lines insurer refuses or is unable to pay legitimate claims; this is seen as causing the broker to be more cautious as to which insurance companies are used. States also generally require that brokers provide specific disclosure statements to clients purchasing surplus lines insurance detailing that the insurance is not subject to the same regulatory oversight as insurance bought from state licensed insurers.

All states levy specific premium taxes on insurance and generally require a licensed insurer to collect and remit these taxes as a condition of licensure. With the absence of licensure requirements on surplus lines insurers, the requirement to remit taxes is placed on the state-licensed broker. The precise amount of the tax depends on individual state laws. The situation becomes somewhat unclear, however, when the consumer, the broker, or the insured property are in different states. Such a multi-state situation requires apportioning the premium taxes among the different states. State laws, however, differ significantly not only on the amount of such taxes but also on what exactly is to be taxed and how that tax should be apportioned among the multiple states.

THE SURPLUS LINES MARKETPLACE

The property/casualty insurance market has been marked by the so-called insurance cycle, a tendency to have alternating periods of high prices and short supply ("hard markets") with periods of low prices and plentiful supply ("soft markets"). The size of the surplus lines market has been significantly affected by these cycles, with surplus lines growing faster than the entire market in hard markets and more slowly in soft markets. In the past 30 years, there have been generally hard markets in four periods: the late 1970s, the middle 1980s, the early 1990s, and the early 2000s. Growth in net premiums for U.S. professional surplus lines insurers in three of these four periods has reached 70% at the peak and then dropped to nearly zero or below within a few years afterwards.[4] In 2008, surplus lines direct premiums totaled $34.4 billion, 13.8% of the total commercial lines premiums of $249.3 billion. The surplus lines market in the United States has two large groups, AIG and Lloyd's of London, which had 23.5% and 19.7% of the market respectively. The next largest is Zurich Financial with 5.0% market share, which was followed by a number of companies in the 2% to 4% range. The 10th-largest company had a 2.1% share, whereas the 20th had a 1.1% market share.[5]

LEGISLATION

109th Congress

The National Insurance Act of 2006 (S. 2509/H.R. 6225)

Senators John Sununu and Tim Johnson introduced S. 2509 on April 5, 2006, and it was referred to the Senate Banking, Housing, and Urban Affairs

Committee. The committee held two hearings on general insurance regulation in July 2006 where the bill was discussed, but it did not take other action on S. 2509. Although not directly addressing surplus lines insurance, the bill could potentially have had a significant impact on the operation of the current surplus lines market. S. 2509 would have created a federal charter for insurers and insurance intermediaries and given them the choice of operating under the federal system instead of the state system. Holders of a federal license would have been able to operate throughout the United States without separate state insurance licenses. In addition, the National Insurance Act would have preempted state laws requiring product and price approvals for federally chartered insurers. A federal charter as envisioned in S. 2509 would thus offer many of the same freedoms currently enjoyed by surplus lines insurers, namely, the ability to sell insurance across the country without individual state licenses and with product and rate flexibility. At the same time, S. 2509 would have offered the possibility of avoiding the conflicting state regulatory system that surplus lines insurers currently point to as a significant burden.

Representative Ed Royce introduced H.R. 6225 on September 28, 2006. It was jointly referred to the House Committees on Financial Services and on the Judiciary. Although not identical to S. 2509, the bill was essentially similar and would have created the same dual regulatory system with both federal and state charters available for insurers and insurance intermediaries. No committee hearings were held on H.R. 6225.

Passage of either version of the National Insurance Act of 2006, however, would not have offered a uniformly positive federal option from the viewpoint of surplus lines insurers. Unlike current state laws for surplus lines insurers, insurers with a federal charter would have been required to participate in state guaranty funds. In addition, federally chartered insurers would likely have had more stringent financial oversight than the states currently undertake with surplus lines insurers. It is difficult to predict whether large numbers of surplus lines insurers would actually opt out of the state system until the details of a federal chartering system were put in place. The largest surplus lines insurer, AIG, would seem very likely to become a national insurer, as its then-chairman testified before Congress supporting an optional federal charter in 2002.[6] A.M. Best's 2006 survey of the surplus lines industry concluded, however, that "whether or not the National Insurance Act becomes a reality, surplus lines insurers will continue to play a major role in providing specialty coverage to commercial insurance consumers."[7]

The Nonadmitted and Reinsurance Reform Act of 2006 (H.R. 5637)

Representative Ginny Brown-Waite, along with 16 cosponsors, introduced H.R. 5637 on June 19, 2006. It was referred to the House Financial Services Committee where hearings were held and the bill amended and reported on to the full House (H.Rept. 109-649). H.R. 5637 was jointly referred to the House Judiciary Committee which held a subcommittee hearing on the bill, but took no further action. On September 27, 2006, the full House took up the bill under Suspension of the Rules and passed it 417-0. The Senate received the bill and referred it to the Banking, Housing, and Urban Affairs Committee, but took no further action.

H.R. 5637 was a relatively narrow bill, aimed directly at streamlining and addressing inconsistencies in state regulation in the surplus lines insurance market. It would have done this primarily through preempting various state laws. It generally would not, however, have replaced the preempted state laws with federal standards, but instead would have done so with laws from other states or model laws of the NAIC. The bill's first two sections would have given preeminent regulatory and tax authority to the home state of the insured, preempting the tax and regulatory laws of other states who might have a claim on the insurance transaction such as the home state of the broker or the location of some of the insured risk. Thus, for example, if a company in one state were purchasing a surplus lines policy that covered some risks in another state, the only state that could collect taxes on that transaction would be the home state of that company. The bill would, however, have allowed states to require reports detailing risks that may be covered by policies from other states as well as encouraged the creation of an interstate compact to develop a uniform formula to allocate surplus lines taxes among the states. H.R. 5637 also would have preempted state laws on eligibility requirements. In general, it would have preempted any state laws that are different from the NAIC's model law on nonadmitted insurance and required states to follow the NAIC's listing of alien insurers in allowing brokers to place insurance with companies from outside of the United States. It also specifically would have preempted state diligent search requirements for surplus lines purchases by "exempt commercial purchasers" as defined in the bill.

H.R. 5637 addressed reinsurance as well as surplus lines insurance. As with the surplus lines provisions, the reinsurance provisions had a similar "home state" approach to addressing inconsistencies of state regulation of reinsurance. The bill would have given preeminence to the home state of the insurer purchasing reinsurance with regard to the regulation of credit for reinsurance and other aspects of the reinsurance contract, while the home state of the reinsurer was given authority for the regulation of solvency of the reinsurer. In order for the home state to be given this primacy, the bill would have required the home state to follow NAIC standards with regard to reinsurance credit and reinsurer solvency.

110th Congress

The Nonadmitted and Reinsurance Reform Act of 2007 (H.R. 1065/S. 929)

Representative Dennis Moore, along with 43 cosponsors, introduced H.R. 1065 on February 15, 2007; Representative Moore was a lead cosponsor of H.R. 5637 in the 109th Congress. Representative Ginny Brown-Waite, the sponsor of H.R. 5637, was a lead cosponsor of the H.R. 1065. H.R. 1065 was nearly identical to the bill that passed the House in the previous Congress. The only change was to the credentials necessary to be considered a "Qualified Risk Manager," which would be required for a company to be considered an "exempt commercial purchaser." The bill was considered under Suspension of the Rules on June 25, 2007, and passed the House by voice vote.

S. 929 also entitled the Nonadmitted and Reinsurance Reform Act of 2007, was introduced in the Senate on March 20, 2007, by Senators Mel Martinez and Bill Nelson. S. 929 was identical to H.R. 5637 as passed by the House during the 109th Congress. It was referred to the Senate Banking, Housing, and Urban Affairs Committee as was H.R. 1065 once it was received in the Senate. Neither bill was acted on by the Senate in the 110th Congress.

The National Insurance Act of 2007 (S. 40/H.R. 3200)

Senators John Sununu and Tim Johnson introduced S. 40 on May 24, 2007, whereas Representative Melissa Bean and Ed Royce introduced H.R. 3200 on July 26, 2007. S. 40/H.R. 3200 were substantially similar to S. 2509/H.R. 6225 from the 109th Congress. They would have created an optional federal charter for the insurance industry, potentially offering surplus lines insurers the choice of continuing to operate under the state system or to do so under the new federal system. Although S. 2509/H.R. 6225 did not specifically address surplus lines insurance, S. 40/H.R. 3200 included provisions doing so. In particular, S. 40/H.R. 3200 included surplus lines insurance under the definition of an "insurance producer" and would have allowed a national agency to sell surplus lines insurance. Thus, under S. 40/H.R. 3200, an individual surplus lines broker or an agency specializing in surplus insurance could hold a national license and be exempt from the various requirements, such as diligent search, placed by the states on surplus lines brokers or agencies. In addition, S. 40/H.R. 3200 would have allowed only the state in which an insured resides or maintains its principal place of business to tax a surplus lines transaction. S. 40/H.R. 3200 would have also specifically exempted surplus lines insurers from a national guaranty fund should one be created. These bills were referred to committee, but no action was taken on them.

111th Congress

The Nonadmitted and Reinsurance Reform Act of 2009 (H.R. 2571/S. 1363/H.R. 4173/S. 3217/P.L. 111-203)

Representative Dennis Moore introduced H.R. 2571 on May 21, 2009, along with 20 cosponsors, including lead cosponsor Representative Scott Garrett. H.R. 2571 is substantially similar to H.R. 1065, which passed the House in the 110th Congress. It was referred to the House Financial Services Committee and Judiciary Committee. Although neither committee marked up the bill, the House took up H.R. 2571 on September 9, 2009, under suspension of the rules and passed the bill by voice vote. Representatives Moore and Garrett also offered the language of H.R. 2571 as a floor amendment to the Wall Street Reform and Consumer Protection Act of 2009 (H.R. 4173). This language was included in an en bloc amendment by Representative Barney Frank (H.Amdt. 529) that passed by voice vote on December 10, 2009. H.R. 4173 passed the House on a vote of 223-202 on December 11, 2009, with the language included as Title IX.

S. 1363, which is identical to H.R. 2571, was introduced in the Senate on June 25, 2009, by Senator Mel Martinez with three cosponsors. It was referred to the Senate Banking, Housing, and Urban Affairs Committee, which has not acted on this bill. The committee did, however, markup and order reported the Restoring America's Financial Stability Act of 2010 on March 22, 2010. Title V, Subtitle B of this bill is entitled the Nonadmitted and Reinsurance Reform Act of 2010 and contains language nearly identical to S. 1363. The bill was reported as S. 3217 on April 15, 2010; after various floor amendments, none of which altered Title V, Subtitle B, the Senate inserted the language of S. 3217 into H.R. 4173 and passed the amended bill on a vote of 59-39.

The conference report on H.R. 4173, now titled the Dodd-Frank Wall Street Reform and Consumer Protection Act, included the Nonadmitted and

Reinsurance Reform Act as Title V, Subtitle B. The House agreed to the conference report on June 30, 2010, by a vote of 237-192 and the Senate agreed to the conference report on July 15, 2010, by a vote of 60-39. President Obama signed the legislation into law as P.L. 111-203 on July 21, 2010.

The National Insurance Consumer Protection Act (H.R. 1880)

H.R. 1880 was introduced by Representatives Melissa Bean and Edward Royce on April 2, 2009. It was referred to the House Financial Services Committee, Judiciary Committee, and Energy and Commerce Committee. This bill includes language similar to the previous National Insurance Act of 2007 that would (1) include surplus lines insurance under the definition of an "insurance producer" and allow a national agency to sell surplus lines insurance and (2) allow only the state in which an insured party resides or maintains its principal place of business to tax a surplus lines transaction. Like previous bills, H.R. 1880 allows for the federal chartering of insurers and insurance producers and loosens some restrictions on insurance rate and form regulation, so it might have an impact on surplus lines insurance as some insurers and producers may choose to become federally chartered, rather than remaining state-chartered surplus lines insurers. The specific provisions of H.R. 1880, however, are different than the previous National Insurance Acts, including the creation of a systemic risk regulation and the provision that some insurers might be required to become federally chartered if judged to be systemically significant.

End Notes

[1] See CRS Report R40771, Insurance Regulation: Issues, Background, and Legislation in the 111th Congress, by Baird Webel, for a more complete overview of insurance regulation.

[2] 15 U.S.C. Sec. 1011 et seq.

[3] P.L. 106-102, 113 Stat. 1338.

[4] A. M. Best, Excess and Surplus 2005, September 2005, p. 19.

[5] Statistics from A. M. Best, U.S. Surplus Lines—Market Review, September 14, 2009, pp. 5-6.

[6] See the statement of M. R. Greenberg before the House Financial Services Subcommittee on Capital Markets, Insurance, and Government Sponsored Enterprises, June 18, 2002, at http://financialservices.house.gov/media/pdf/ 061802mg.pdf.

[7] A.M. Best, Surplus Lines Market 2006, September 2006, p. 27.

INDEX

D

E

F

G

H

I

N

O

P

Q

R

S

T

U

V

W